Black Faggot
and other plays

Black Faggot
and other plays

Victor Rodger

Victoria University Press

VICTORIA UNIVERSITY PRESS
Victoria University of Wellington
PO Box 600 Wellington
vup.victoria.ac.nz

ISBN 9781776561032

A catalogue record for this book is available from the National Library
of New Zealand.

Printed by Ligare, Auckland

Contents

Black Faggot

In 2004 Destiny Church organised a march against the Civil Union Bill. They marched to protect the sanctity of marriage between a man and a woman.

Fathers marched with sons. Watching them, I knew in my heart that, at the *very least,* one of those sons would be gay and feeling wretched about his sexuality. You would too if you were essentially marching against yourself.

With that in mind I began to write what would become *Black Faggot.* It was my way of saying to that hypothetical kid that it was all going to be alright.

I wrote the cornerstone monologues in 2006: young Christian on the Enough is Enough march; the unaplogetic Semu dishing it out to some homophobes; James trying to convince his straight mate he knows how to eat pussy. After that the project stalled, until in 2012 opposition from some members of the Pacific community to the Marriage Equality Bill began to get a bit loud. That gave me the motivation to finally finish the play.

Black Faggot debuted in February 2013. Two months later Parliament voted to allow same-sex marriage. The sky did not fall in, as had been predicted; the very fabric of society was not ripped asunder.

I turned up to the opening night of *Black Faggot* a little apprehensive. I imagined the language and sexual situations described in the play were enough to give some people coronaries. And yet the play got a standing ovation and *Black Faggot* went on to become my most successful play to date.

It's been performed throughout New Zealand as well as in

Australia and Edinburgh, and, at the time of writing, is about to be staged in Honolulu.

Straight white middle-class audiences have lapped it up. Even one of my deeply Catholic Samoan aunties found herself chuckling along with the rest of the audience.

Of all the reviews, the one that's really moved me came from a young, gay, mixed-race man in Palmerston North.

'Are you the writer?' he asked me in the lobby of Centrepoint Theatre after the closing night performance. I nodded. 'Mean,' he said. He explained that he worked at a fast-food outlet in Palmerston North. That this was his second time watching the play.

'Thank you for writing this,' he said. 'This is, like, my story.'

As much as I'd like to, I can't take all the credit for *Black Faggot*. The original cast, Iaheto Ah Hi and Beulah Koale, did some terrific improvisations which found their ways in to the finished script. Long-time friend but first-time theatre producer Karin Williams probably initially wondered what the hell she'd signed on for, but she helped keep the *Black Faggot* train moving, nationally and internationally. The director, Roy Ward, especially helped *Black Faggot* become what it was. He gave the play two things it didn't possess when we started rehearsals: a narrative and, more importantly, a heart. Both were crucial to its success.

Ia manuia,

Victor Rodger

I never understood what it took to love another man until I was transformed by the love of another man. I would come to be with many men in my life. The one man I've learnt to keep loving every day is still myself. *Black Faggot* reminds us all that we are capable of enduring great pain, trudging through life's despicable ironies. And that on the other side of all that pain and fear we are also capable of experiencing real love. The type of love that saves our lives.

—Tanu Gago, queer activist and artistic director, FAF SWAG

For Roy Ward

Black Faggot premiered in 2013 at the Basement Theatre in Auckland. It was produced by Karin Williams for Multinesia Productions, with the following cast and production team:

Staunch and others	Iaheto Ah Hi
Undercover Brother and others	Beulah Koale

Developed in association with Roy Ward.

Director	Roy Ward
Lighting Designer	Jennifer Lal

Black Faggot

Staunch (Semu) is about to speak when . . .

Punk: Black faggot!

Staunch: And what? And what? Come on then. Bring it on, motherfucker, bring it. Yeah, I'm a black faggot. And what? And what? Tell me something I don't know. Come on, surprise me. Whatcha got? Whatcha got?

Punk: BLACK HOMO!

Staunch: Oh, I'm a black homo now? Is that it? Is that all you got? So first I was a black faggot and now I'm a black homo? S-A-D sad one, man. Already dealing in synonyms, and we've only just begun. Shame. Shame on your inability to express yourself in a more original, compelling fashion. That shows a distinct lack of oral flair. It also indicates something I suspected from the start: that you're a thick black shit.

Punk: What?

Staunch: Are you deaf? I said: that you're a THICK BLACK SHIT. Tell you what: I'll take black faggot over thick black shit any day. And I'll tell you something else: bananas are on special at Pak'nSave so why don't you baboons fuck off and get a feed before I kick all your sorry asses to the end of never! Yeah, I'm a black faggot. Re-cog-nise! Yea-yah!

*

Christian: (*chanting*) Enough is enough! Enough is enough!
Enough is enough! Enough is . . . Ow, my arm, I
think I sprained it or something. It's all this punching
in the air. Man, I could do with a rub, that's for sure.
Might be a rotator-cuff injury. Gosh, is it me or is it
really hot?

*He rolls the sleeves of his T-shirt up and ties the bottom
of the T-shirt into a knot.*

That's better. Here, do you want me to help you with
your . . . ? Okay, just a*k*sing, no need to bite my head
off, my gosh, it was just a question. I hate getting
all sweaty, y'know, like, when it trickles down your
back and slides into your undies. How much further
do we have to walk anyway? My calves are *killing*
me. I was going to wear my Nikes but I thought it
would be better for my look if I wore these dress
shoes with a heel, just in case I get on TV, what do
you think? Dang, it's hot. I just feel like taking this
off altogether. Whose great idea was it to wear black
anyway? Stink, man. Black attracts heat, everyone
knows that. We should've done this in white.
Would've looked nicer too. Yeah, and then I could've
worn my Lonsdale track pants, nine bucks from Foot
Locker, I got that friends and family discount, you
should see them, they're off the hook. You can see
my undies through them, though, but that doesn't
matter, eh? Hey, did you see those two guys kissing?
Man, they were going hard out, like really getting
stuck into each other. So disgusting. I was like, Adam
and Eve not Adam and Steve, enough is enough,
alright? I mean, you could see their tongues and
everything and they were rubbing their hands all over
each other's butts, like this.

He demonstrates.

Just . . . so . . . gross. And did you see what they were
wearing? Like hardly anything. Just these short little
shorts that were cut all the way up to here and they
had these rings in their nipples.

He circles his nipples with his fingers.

Enough is enough, man! I talked to them for a
while and tried to tell them how being gay was a sin
and how they'll go to hell if they don't stop doing
each other up the back door and—get this. Do you
know what they said to me? They said I was the
biggest faggot they'd ever seen in their lives. Isn't that
ridiculous?

He laughs loudly then suddenly stops.

Well, it is ridiculous. Totally ridiculous.

Pause.

Enough is enough! Enough is enough!

*

*Mama Letti (Undercover Brother's mother) is watching
TV.*

Mama Letti: Oi James, sau. Vave. Your cousin Christian is on the
TV. Awww, doesn't he look cute? Enough is enough,
alright. Ia, good on them. Good on them standing up
to the gays. And good on that Brian Tamaki, uh? Oi,
I like the way he does his hair.

Bro (Undercover Brother's brother): Shhhht. James? Did you
spill something on my *Rugby News*? I wanted to read
that article on Sonny Bill Williams but it's all stuck
together. What'd you spill on it? Told you about
reading my shit when you've got dirty hands.

He smells the magazine.

Wait—what the . . . ? Is that . . . ?

He smells again; recognises the smell.

Fucking James!

*

FOB Dad: James?

Undercover Brother: Yes, Dad?

FOB Dad: Have you been on my computer today?

Undercover Brother: Um. Yeah.

FOB Dad: You wanna explain something to me?

Undercover Brother: Sure. What?

FOB Dad: When I clicked on the 'History' button to find my poker website I noticed someone had been on another website today. A website called *bigblackcocks.com*. Son, what are you looking up big black cocks for on my computer?

Undercover Brother: Oh it's, um, for this assignment we have to do at school.

FOB Dad: An assignment?

Undercover Brother: Yeah. About chickens.

FOB Dad: Chickens?

Undercover Brother: Yeah. Chickens. Well, cocks. The male chickens.

FOB Dad: Son, I know what a cock is, thank you very much.

Undercover Brother: I just wanted you to be clear so you weren't confused or any—

FOB Dad: Why do you need to look up big black cocks?

Undercover Brother: Um, because, uh, the assignment, it's about minority chickens living in a white chicken world and about the oppression they face in a Eurocentric context.

Beat.

FOB Dad: Ia, ok. Good boy, James. Go make your father a cup of Milo.

*

Fa'afāfine Artist (Miranda Malo): Ladies and gentlemen, minister, esteemed colleagues: warm Pacific greetings. And when I say warm, I mean warm. Especially to that fine brother in the back row. Mmmmhmmmm, yes, brother, you. No, not you. Hell, no. The one next you in the mustard. Yeah, you (*winks*). Most of you will already know me, but for those of you who do not, please allow me to introduce my own self: My name is Miranda Malo and I am a multiple award-winning fa'afāfine—recognised third sex—artist, originally from Samoa, internationally recognised for my provocative works, such as 'Ass You Like It' and 'Me, Myself, My Muli'. The first work I'd like to discuss tonight is 'Undercover Brother'—a sculpture which explores the concept of the Polynesian brother who is on the down-low. A man who sometimes has sex with other men but keeps it secret from everyone. His family. His church. His friends. Even, sometimes, his own wife or girlfriend. If accused of engaging in any gay behaviour, the Undercover Brother will vigorously deny it. I give you: 'Undercover Brother'.

*

Mate: You're a homo, eh?

Undercover Brother: Doubt it. I'm not, man. Come on. As if. Are you serious? I love pussy, man. Pussy is the shit. I mean, it's like double Y to the U to the M, man: Yum. Yum. Can't eat enough of it. Even better than KFC. I could eat it all day long. I wish I could put it in my sandwiches and take it to work for lunch, that's how much I like to eat it.

Mate: When's the last time you had some?

Undercover Brother: I get it all the time, bro.

Mate: Never seen you eat pussy.

Undercover Brother: Yeah, well just 'cause you don't see me eating pussy, doesn't mean I don't. Fah, man. Besides, if you actually saw me eating it that'd just be wrong. Hey— maybe *you're* a faggot. Yeah, that's right, maybe you're a . . .

Mate: What does it taste like then?

Undercover Brother: You clown. Don't you know? Is that why you're asking?

Mate: You don't know.

Undercover Brother: 'Course I know. What a sad guy. Bro, I got nothing to prove, a'ite? You don't know what pussy tastes like, that's your own damn problem, fool.

Mate: What's it taste like then?

Undercover Brother: Fah, okay then. It tastes like. Um. Honey. Yeah, honey. Sweet. Really sweet. Like candy. (*sings*) 'I'll take you to the candy shop.' Yeah, that's what I'm talkin' about. Well, no—what I mean is, it tastes like honey and it's sweet like candy but it, y'know, still tastes like . . . whatever, this conversation is . . .

Mate: How do you eat it?

Undercover Brother: (*nervous laugh*) How do I . . . how do I *what*? Are you for reals? I'm not going to tell you that, man. That shit is out of line. That's just sick . . . like, sick. Puke sick. Fah, man.

Mate: Hurry up, cunt!

Undercover Brother: Oh alright, alright. Like this.

          He demonstrates licking pussy in an exaggerated fashion.

          Okay? Satisfied now? I just showed you, didn't I?

Mate: What do you do with your fingers?

Undercover Brother: What the hell? Are you on crack? Fah, man. I just . . . y'know . . .

He delicately demonstrates pulling the lips of a vagina apart.

. . . and then . . .

He demonstrates licking pussy again.

Mate: What about her titties?

Undercover Brother: Well, I . . . I just . . . reach on up . . .

He reaches up one hand and pretends to tweak a titty.

. . . and go like that. Tweak, tweak. Drives 'em crazy, like, out of their minds.

Mate: How do you fuck her?

Undercover Brother: No, bro, that's it. This is like, too out of it. I'm not telling you, bro. Bro, I'm serious.

Mate: Hurry up.

Undercover Brother: Fah, man, Okay . . . well . . . when we get down to it I just . . . slide on in and go hard out for, like, a few hours and, yeah. It's awesome. Satisfied now?

Mate: One more thing.

Undercover Brother: Fah, man, alright, but this is the last question. I mean it, bro, no more.

Mate: What's up with that picture you got of Sonny Bill Williams in your room?

Undercover Brother: What picture of Sonny Bill Williams? Oh. That one on my ceiling? I put it up there for inspiration. 'Cause I want to be an All Black.

Mate: Since when?

Undercover Brother: Like, since forever, you dick. Why else would I have a poster of Sonny Bill Williams in his undies on my ceiling? Fah, man. Out of it.

*

Staunch: Oi sole, sounds like you had a bomb-as weekend with that chick, alright. Good on you, bro. I tapped me some too, y'know? It was wicked. He was this fine as brother with cornrows and . . . Excuse me? No, no, no, no, no: fair's fair, bro. I listened to you go on about how you whacked your cock against that chick's face then came all over her tits. Did I tell you to shut up? No, I did not. Did I say, 'Ooooh, gross, he's talking about fucking some chick's pussy'? No, I did not. You know why? Because my mother raised me to have manners. I listened to your story 'cause it's manners, bro. And because you're my mate. So now it's only fair that you listen to me. Alright? I mean, you're my mate, right? So mates listen to each other. Alright? Okay. So. I was at the club, busting my moves—and y'know, when Flo Rida came on I was like, yes, yes, yo, and so I'm giving it some of this and that.

He does some moves.

And then I look across the floor and there he is: this fine chocolate piece of mmmmm, tall . . . dark—not too dark, just dark enough—bubble butt, pecs like 'Oooh yeah', and he looked over at me and then he smiled and then I was like, Damn, he's a Tongan. He had a mouthful of gold in there, man, but he was still fine, so I give him the (*flicks his eyebrows up*) and then we get talking, and one thing lead to another and next thing we're back at my place and this guy is a freak, man, he's like licking my balls like they're Scorched Almonds or something, and then he gets all my lollipop in his mouth—never seen that before,

bro, never—and then he's like, 'I want you to pound
my ass to the end of never.' Bet you never had a chick
say that to you, uh? And I'm like . . . Hey, where's
your manners, man, I'm not finished. And what's
with that ill look? You're just jealous, man. Anyway,
where was I? Yeah, 'I want you to pound my ass to
the end of never,' and I'm like, 'Damn, you don't
have to tell me twice, sole,' so we get butt naked and
ka-boo-yah, I slide on in there and I'm like—

He mimics fucking the guy.

—nice and slow to start with and this guy is moaning
like a motherfucker, and then I (*he speeds up*) and
he's like 'Oh yeah, oh yeah,' and I was just going
hard out, getting right up inside that brother until I
couldn't take it anymore and, oh, bro, you shoulda
seen me shoot. Went all the way across the room, out
the window and onto the neighbour's fence. So, yeah,
that was my weekend.

*

Christian sings 'This Little Light of Mine'.

He sings the first verse straight . . .

*But on the second verse he starts to let loose, and by the end of the song
it's like he's in a Beyoncé video, twerking and jerking . . .*

. . . Until he realises everyone is looking.

*Self-conscious, Christian reverts back to being straight . . . And
ashamed . . .*

*

> *Darkness. Moaning. Lights up on Anal Queen, on his
> back, legs up in the air. And then:*

Anal Queen (Alien): Oh my God, Michael, you just came on the
duvet? Why'd you come on the duvet? You know I
just put that cover on today. Hello: I'm going to have

to clean it now, because of you and your goo, thanks a lot. God. Yes, I know you got excited, Michael. Of course you got excited. I'm an amazing lover. I get it. But why did you have to get excited all over the fa-rickin' duvet? Why couldn't you just come in your hand or grab that lavalava? Next time just say 'Yo, I'm about to shoot,' flip onto your back and come on yourself? Hey presto, no man-yoghurt on the duvet. None of this 'coming wherever you feel like it' shit, I mean what do you think the world would be like, Michael, if we just came all over the place wherever we felt like it? In the sink. On the floor. On the curtains?

He realises the curtains are open and hurriedly shuts them.

What the hell do you think you're doing? Move that muli. I need to clean this shit up. Yes, right now. No, Michael, we can most certainly not just lie here and spoon. God, you really do think it's all about you, don't you? Outrageous.

*

Kid in Class (10): My brother Rob. My brother's name is Rob but we all call him Alien. My sister says we call him Alien because he acts like he is from another planet. My brother lives with his palagi friend Michael in the city. They are really really good friends because they only have one bed in their apartment and they both sleep in it. My mum said it's because they can't afford two beds but when she said that my sister started laughing and then she choked on her sapasui and blew some out of her nose. That was really funny. When my brother Rob and his palagi friend Michael come home for ko'ogai sometimes they are really tired. One time they were so tired they fell asleep outside in their car. Mum said it was because they had been working hard but my sister said it's because they went to Family. Family is this place in the city. I think it is called Family because people can take their families there but Rob has never taken us there. Maybe one day we will all go to Family. The end.

*

Hustler (Sione): What are you to-ing? I said: what are you to-ing? Chee, ton't you speak English? Fea le keige? I said where's your kirlfriend? Oi, sole. Leai se girlfriend? A handsome man like you, single? Or does that mean you kot a poyfriend? Nah, just jokey joke, don't get n-n-n-nasty. I'm Sione. Nice to meet you. I'm from Samoa. You ever peen to Samoa? You would love it there. It's hot and it's peautiful. Just like me. Oi, I love this song. 'It's Pritney, pitch'. Pritney Spears, she so sexy. T-Chay, turn that shit up! To you wanna tance? I said: To you wanna tance? I love to tance. You wanna see me tance? I can tance like Michael Jackson. See?

He does a bit of Michael.

Or you wanna see me do the 'Gangnam Style'?

He dances the 'Hey, sexy lady' bit.

Or how about I tance like Beyoncé?

He dances a bit of 'Single Ladies'.

Oi sole, ton't poop the party. Come on, tance, tance with me. Come on. We'll have good times. E aikae, then. (*to another man*) Oi, what are you to-ing?

*

Staunch: What kind of dumb ass question is that? 'Why do I want to be gay?' Well, why you want to be straight? You just do, right? You don't even think about it. Sheeze-us. Same with cock. I want to lick some guy's balls, it's all Nike, bro: Just Do It. It's not a choice. Nigga, please: who in their right mind would choose to deal with all that shit. Church. Homophobia. People who can't spell. Did you see those Tongans when they were protesting against the marriage equality bill? 'All MPs support gay/lesbis law are Mantally sick MPs.' Mantally sick. That's what my dad said when I came out: It's a choice. I said to him, The choice would be for me to get with a girl and pretend I was straight—like your nephew Aaron. I used to see him on the scene all the time giving his muli up for anything with a pulse. Suddenly he's married with kids and you know he ain't surrendered that side of himself but there he is, accepted into the fold. Because he's toeing the line.

You want to talk about choice. *That*'s the choice.

*

Staunch: Sup, sole?

Undercover Brother: Oh, uh, malo.

Staunch: Haven't seen you here before.

Undercover Brother: I just came in to use the toilet and grab a water.

Staunch: Where you from?

Undercover Brother: Out south. Sole, is this a gay bar?

Staunch: Uh-huh. So what do you think?

Undercover Brother: It's different. The music is pretty whack.

Staunch: True that. You know the one thing that makes me wish I was straight? The music at gay bars. Why they always play this white-boy gay shit? You know what I mean? They'll have someone up on the turntables who can't spin for shit, and what they're spinning . . . forget about it. You heard of DJ Love

It? DJ Fucken Hate It. But get this. It's even worse
in Christchurch. We go to this club back in the day
and they're playing some sad piece of Kylie, *oons-oons*,
and we're the only niggas there and I go up to the DJ,
this old palagi fulla who looks like he's a 100 years
old and I go, Can you can you play something black,
please? And he's, like, all *Fear of a Black Planet* and he
goes, This is a gay club. And I'm like, Well, there are
black gay people too. And he looks at me like I just
pissed in his mother's mouth and goes: Oh, alright
then. I'll play Scribe.

Fucking Christchurch.

Undercover Brother: Fah, what an angry guy. You always that
angry?

Staunch: No. Not always. Semu.

Undercover Brother: Jay.

Staunch: Nice to meet you, Jay . . .

They shake hands.

*

Old Rich White Guy: Welcome, welcome. Bienvenue. What do
your people say?

Hustler: Afio mai?

Old Rich White Guy: Ooooh, are you sure that's not your name?
Afio mai?

Hustler: Sione.

Old Rich White Guy: Yes, I know it's Sione. It's always Sione. If I
had a dollar—or should I say 'tala'? Ha ha ha. Fancy
a drink? I've got a lavalava out back if you want to
slip into something more comfy. You like that, do
you? It's by Miranda Malo. She's a Samoan. She's a
fa'afāfine. It's a lovely little piece of work, don't you
think? Sometimes I look at it and I can just smell the

frangipani.

Hustler: Toilet.

Old Rich White Guy: It's just over there.

He keeps a nervous eye on him.

No, you've gone too far. Yes, that one. (*yells*) I don't often bring strangers home. Seriously. Can't be too careful these days, can you?

Hustler: Hungry.

Old Rich White Guy: Well, I've got some crackers and cheese and . . .

Hustler: Chicken.

Old Rich White Guy: Well, yes, I do have some chicken but it's in the freezer. I'd have to throw it in the microwave to defrost it and then . . .

Hustler: Pleeeeeeease.

Old Rich White Guy: Oh, fine, no, not a problem, I bring you home at three in the morning, it's no problem to cook for you, no problem at all. How about I cook some free range eggs instead and throw some organic bacon under the grill and . . .

Hustler: Fried.

Old Rich White Guy: You don't really want it fried, do you? You'll get fat and develop diabetes if you carry on like that. Tell you what, I can think of something else you might like to eat and you certainly won't develop diabetes from that. Have a guess. Go on.

Hustler: What?

Old Rich White Guy: No, have a guess.

Hustler: What?

Old Rich White Guy: JESUS CHRIST, HAVE A GUESS. FIRST

THING THAT POPS INTO YOUR HEAD.
THERE, THAT'S A CLUE. HEAD, GET IT? Never
mind, it was just an idea. Maybe later. How do you
have your eggs?

*

Kid (10): Uppercut? Why I gotta learn how to uppercut?

Father: Because you need to learn how to be a man.

Kid: This is boring. I wanna go home and watch *Project Runway*. When I grow up I wanna be just like Michael Kors.

Father: Who?

Kid: Michael Kors. Dad, don't you know anything?

Father: Sssht. Enough about *Project Runaway*. Stay behind the jab. Come on. Use your right hand. Straight down the middle. Now move out of the corner— fight your way out—don't take the shots! Now, move around the ring! Move. Don't go too hard. Pace yourself. Okay, now grab the rope. Don't skip like a girl! Skip like a man. Push yourself, son!

Kid: It hurts.

Father: I know it hurts, son. Stop crying. Now try that uppercut again. Attack.

Kid: But why?

Father: Because your dad's going to teach you how to take care of yourself if it's the last thing he does. Come on, hurry up.

Father throws the rope at Kid. Kid throws it back. Father looks like he could hit the Kid.

*

Christian: Hi, God. How are you? It's Christian here. But you already know that, right? Since you know everything.

Actually, since you know everything then, you know what I'm going to say, right? So does that mean I still have to say it, even though you already know it?

Beat.

The thing is: I think I'm gay, God. Actually I don't think I am. I know I am. I think I've known ever since I was a kid. Sorry about that, God. I know you're not into gays and stuff. But guess what? Neither am I. I don't want to be like this. I want to be like everyone else. The way you want me to be. Anyway, my cousin Letitia, she said you can pray the gay away, so what I was wondering, Lord, was: can you please make me not gay anymore? Please? I'm sick of people calling me a black faggot. And I don't want to go to hell. And 'cause you know everything, you know the way my dad looks at me, eh God? Like he wishes I wasn't his son. Maybe, when I'm not gay anymore, he won't give me that look anymore, eh God? That'd be wicked. Anyway, thanks for listening, God. See you soon.

*

Darkness. Moaning. Lights up on Anal Queen on all fours. And then:

Anal Queen: Oh my God, Michael, you just came on the wallpaper. Why'd you come on the wallpaper? Look at it: it's everywhere. Yes, I know told you to flip over onto your back next time, but did I or did I not specifically instruct you to come on your stomach, not all over the damn wallpaper. You needed to hold your dick towards you like this (*demonstrates*) not up in the fa-rickin air like that (*demonstrates*). Didn't you learn anything about angles when you were in high school? God, Michael. That wallpaper is made out of fabric. Not vinyl. Fabric. It's not jizz-resistant. It won't just wipe off. Do you even know how much it cost? And now you put your spoof all over it! What do you think mum's going to say when she sees this? You know what she's like; she was born with blacklight vision. She'll be like, 'What's that?' Why are you laughing? God, you really do think it's all about you, don't you? Outrageous.

*

Liberal: Kia ora, talofa lava, fakalofa lahi atu, mālō e lelei, bula vinaka, kia orana, taloha ni. My name is Vili and it's my privilege to be here today in your school to discuss homophobia. Can anyone tell me what homophobia is? Homophobia is when people react negatively to gay people and sometimes call them names. Hurtful names. What are some of the derogatory names that you can think of to describe gay men? It's okay to giggle.

Student: Fairy.

Liberal: Good.

Student: Pillow biter.

Liberal: Excellent.

Student: Ass bandit?

Liberal: Excellent. Anyone else?

Student: Shirt-lifting queer?

Liberal: Uh-uh.

Student: Fudge-packing homo?

Liberal: Very good. Yep, any oth . . . ?

Student: Cock-sucking faggot?

Liberal: We're really getting into the hard stuff, aren't we?

Student: Poo-pusher.

Liberal: I think those are enough terms for us to look at.

Student: Cock-gobbler. Pole-smoker. Turd-burgler.

Liberal: Yeah, okay, I think we'll leave it there, thanks. Let's move on . . .

*

Teen Brother: That film was gay.

Staunch: Hey, you little shit, what did you just say? That that film was 'gay'?

Teen Brother: I didn't mean gay.

Staunch;   Okay, so if you didn't mean that it was gay, what did you say it was gay for then?

Teen Brother: Everyone says gay at school.

Staunch;   I don't give a big black shit what all the other kids are saying at school. I'm your brother, I'm gay and I find it offensive that you are using the word 'gay' to denote something negative.

Teen Brother: Denote?

Staunch: Look it up, fool. How would you like it if I called everything that I thought sucked 'straight'? 'Oh that film was so straight'; 'Don't be such a straight cunt'; 'Ooooh, you straight'. Remember what we discussed at the family meeting? Tolerance, Joshua, tolerance. You better watch it, uso, or I'm going to come to your next assembly wearing my 'I Love Dick' T-shirt and then give a talk about how I'm your brother and how much I love being gay and sucking cock.

Teen Brother: You wouldn't.

Staunch: Wouldn't I? Go on. Try me. Alright then. So just remember: next time you want to say something's gay—find another fucken adjective. Re-cog-nise. Yea-yah!

*

Staunch: Jay? Sup?

Undercover Brother: Oh, hey.

Staunch: Back for another water?

Undercover Brother: Yeah.

Staunch: Pretty good water round here, right?

Beat.

Listen. It's a miracle.

Undercover Brother: What?

Staunch: They're playing a good song. Wanna dance?

Undercover Brother: Oh, nah, I'm sweet, bro.

Staunch: You sure?

Undercover Brother: I don't dance, bro.

Staunch dances.

Old school. My uncle dances like that.

Staunch: How old is your uncle?

Undercover Brother: How old are you?

Staunch: Show me how you do it south-side. Come on then.

Undercover Brother: We don't do those octopus moves. We bounce. Like this.

Undercover Brother begins to dance with Staunch.

The song stops. They look at each other.

*

Old Homo: When I was a kid my father caught me kissing another boy. He took off his belt and beat me back into the closet for thirty years. Thirty years I swallowed who I was. I look at the young ones in the club now. Not a care in the world other than finding

their next drink, their next kiss. They're lucky. Most
of them don't know how lucky they are.

*

Honky Lover/Sexual Tourist speak simultaneously . . .

Sexual Tourist: You're going to Samoa? Oh, you lucky buggar.
Take me with you. Is it hard to pick up? Please. It's as
simple as A-B-see you in my ass. All you do is . . . you
sit along the sea wall in Apia. You wait until someone
sits down next to you. They ask what you're doing.
You giggle like a girl. You say: I'm waiting for a
friend. Buy them a crate of Vailima. And voilà.

Honky Lover: Shame, man, you see Vai on Saturday? He was all
over that fat gorilla. Old enough to be his father.
Actually it sort of looked like his uncle, you know
the one who works at Fisher and Paykel? Man, you
won't catch me near monkey meat. What's wrong
with the brothers? 'Cause it's like . . . too close to
home, yo. Plus they never have any money, man.
It's always, Oh, can you get us a bourbon and Coke,
fa'amolemole. A triple. On the way home: Can
we please stop in at BK? Triple cheeseburger meal,
fa'amolemole. Supersize. Fuck, supersize *this*. What
do I look like? An ATM? Give me a palagi any day.

*. . . Until Honky Lover stops to listen to Sexual
Tourist . . .*

Sexual Tourist: Next thing you know you've got your pants round
your ankles and you're getting fucked in the ass like
there was no tomorrow as you brace yourself against a
palm tree. Bon voyage.

And then Sexual Tourist stops to listen to Honky Lover.

Honky Lover: So what if they can't dance and they're no good in
bed? It don't matter. But as for the brothers? Pfffft.
Forget it.

*

Christian: Father God, I know all things are possible through
you, Lord. So please, Lord, hear my prayer. You know
how there's that whole 'ask and ye shall receive' bit
in the Bible? I'm not trying to hurry you up, God—
cause I know you do things in your own time—but
y'know when I asked if you could make me straight?
I was sorta hoping I might wake up like that in the
morning. Only I didn't. But you already know that,
right? That's alright, God. In your own time. God, I
got one more question: Why'd you make me like this
if you don't even like me being this way? That bit I
really don't get, God. See ya.

*

*Darkness. Moaning. Lights up on Anal Queen giving
head. And then:*

Anal Queen: Oh my God, Michael, you didn't come. Why didn't
you come? What's wrong? I feel like I've been sucking
your dick for a day and a half.

He massages his jaw.

My jaw. My God, it feels dislocated. (*listens*) What
do you mean you were too scared to come? And how
can you even say that after I practically just gave
myself lockjaw sucking your dick? Baby, that's ancient
history. It's all forgotten now. We've moved on.
Besdies, I managed to get most of it off the wallpaper
anyway. I'm sorry, baby. I didn't mean to make you
feel self-conscious or uncomfortable. Okay, so maybe
I was being a little, y'know, anal, but . . . Babe?
Where are you going? Babe? Come back.

Babe?

*

Kid in Class (10): My brother Rob isn't living with his palagi friend Michael anymore. Now he has the bed all to himself. I bet my brother Rob is really happy about that. The end.

*

Fa'afafine Artist: The second work I would like to discuss tonight is 'Cracker Wanna Poly'. The title is, of course, a play on the old phrase 'Polly want a cracker'; a phrase most people take as meaning a parrot by the name of Polly wanting to eat a cracker, as in a biscuit. However, in this instance, Polly is spelt P-O-L-Y, as in Polynesian, and the term Cracker is taken from the southern-state American term for poor white trash. For example, 'Listen here, you po' white cracker.' Thus, instead of Polly the parrot wanting to eat a cracker, we have a cracker—a white man—wanting to eat (*in speech marks*) a Poly—a Polynesian. 'Cracker Wanna Poly' is a response to years of art which has sexualized men and women of colour through the white gaze of white artists, and subverts this by having the Polynesian figure completely clothed while the palagi figure kneels naked at his feet on all fours. Thus the power paradigm shifts from its traditional space with the palagi and moves the power over to the Polynesian, who stands proud. Please note that though the palagi has his face tilted up to look at the Polynesian, the Polynesian's face is turned away, almost as if to say: leai fa'afetai. No, thank you.

*

Hustler: Hello, Tim?

Old Rich White Guy: Sione? Hello. This is a nice surprise to hear from you. Did you enjoy your eggs last night?

Hustler: Yeah, thank you for the eggs.

Old Rich White Guy: Listen, Sione, I don't suppose you happened to gather up my wallet by mistake last night, did you? I can't seem to find it.

Hustler: If I saw it I would have told you. Listen, Tim, I just got the worst news of my life. My mother, she just died.

Old Rich White Guy: Oh, that's awful.

Hustler: She had a heart attack. And now I gotta take her body back to Samoa, but it's just me and her in my family.

Old Rich White Guy: You don't have other family who could help you?

Hustler: I'm a one child.

Old Rich White Guy: What about your mum?

Hustler: She's a one child too.

Old Rich White Guy: Oh, you poor thing.

Hustler: I need a pig favour.

Old Rich White Guy: A pig favour? Oh, a big favour?

Hustler: Please, Tim, I really need some money. I can pay you back when I get to Samoa. Please, Tim, you are one of the most special men I ever meet. Never meet anyone like you.

Old Rich White Guy: Thank you, Sione. But I only met you yesterday.

Hustler: Please, Tim. Can you help me?

Old Rich White Guy: Well, how much do you need?

Hustler: Five thousand dollars.

Old Rich White Guy: That's a lot of money, Sione.

Hustler: I can pay you back as soon as I get to Samoa. Please, Tim, you're the only one who can help me. If you can find it in your heart, fa'amolemole.

Old Rich White Guy: What's your account number?

Hustler: 02629117300.

*

Staunch: Jay? What are you waiting for? Come in.

                     Undercover Brother hesitates.

                     You know that first night I saw you? Standing at the
                     bar? You reminded me of me back in the day. That
                     undercover brother at the bar, all by himself, waiting
                     for something to happen but at the same time scared
                     that it would. Are you scared now?

Undercover Brother: A little.

Staunch: Don't be.

                     Staunch moves in for a kiss.

                     Undercover Brother moves away.

                     What's wrong?

Undercover Brother: My real name. It's not Jay. It's James.

Staunch: Well, malo James. Pleased to meet you.

                     They kiss. Staunch turns to the audience.

                     Samoan men are the most beautiful men in the
                     world.

*

                     Sione is living it up with a girl.

Hustler: Hey, babe, you want another drink? Waiter, can we
                     get another drink, please, for me and my girl?

                     His phone rings. He answers it.

Hustler: Oh hey, Tim. What are you to-ing?

Old Rich White Guy: How are you, Sione?

Hustler: It's peen really busy with the funeral, uh?

Old Rich White Guy: I bet. You poor thing. How much longer are you going to be in Samoa?

Hustler: There's a lot of stuff to sort out first. Could be weeks. Months.

Old Rich White Guy: That's really interesting you say that, Sione. Because I'm looking at you right now from across the road.

Sione looks around, sees Old Rich White Guy.

Hustler: But I'm in Samoa.

Old Rich White Guy: I can see you!

Hustler: You're breaking up, Tim. Gotta go. Fa!

Hustler hangs up and runs away.

Old Rich White Guy: You little shit!

*

Undercover Brother: (*butch voice*) Sup, it's James. (*voice softens*) Hey, Semu. What's up? How you doing? Oh man, I'm all good. Especially after last night. Oh, hang on? I've got another call, just a sec.

He takes another call in his butch voice.

James here. Yeah, uso, all good, eh? What time's practice? Shot. See you then, nigga. Ia fa.

He returns to Semu.

Sorry, about that. Sooooo, last night was off the hook. Like, that was some intense shit. Hang on, I got another call.

He takes another call in his butch voice.

Hi, Mum. Yes, Mum, I can take you to housie. Just hang on a minute, I'm on another call.

He returns to Semu.

I gotta go, it's Mum. But I can't wait to see you again tonight for round two. That thing you did with your tongue, y'know? When you licked my muli . . . ? Man, that was insane.

He laughs. But then there's silence.

Mum? Is that you?

*

Mama Letti: My James. He always got the girls around him, my poy. So popular wif da girls. But I say don't you get up to the mischief with those girls and have a pregnant. You're too young. But he's so handsome. And that's why I don't like him to play rugby with those other apes. They might hurt my beautiful son, his beautiful face, so beautiful, just like his mother. James not like his brother. His brother always hard, like to smash things. Smash, smash, smash. James, when he was a boy, he love butterflies. Love to chase them. Love to flap his little arms and pretend he have butterfly wings. Love to use my hairbrush like a microphone and sing about being a pretty butterfly. Oi, and you should have seen the time he try and pinch his cousin Tasi's fairy wings at her birthday party, kalofa e. I wonder if he remember that? People ask me why James hasn't got a girlfriend yet. I tell them it's just because James is pisi. Too pisi for a girlfriend. Plenty of time.

*

Undercover Brother: What?

Staunch: 'This is Semu? He's my mate'? 'My mate'? Fuck you, James.

Undercover Brother: Those were my boys.

Staunch: You're ashamed of me.

Undercover Brother: You know how it goes.

Staunch: Yeah, I do, undercover brother. Keep it on the down-low 'cause you don't have the nuts to be honest with yourself. Pussy.

Undercover Brother: Shut up.

Staunch: It's true, isn't it?

Undercover Brother: Man, why you gotta be so angry all the time?

Staunch: 'Cause I'm a bit old to go back in the closet. What are you scared of? Haters gonna hate, nigga. Fucking grow a pair.

Undercover Brother: And just go: 'Hey, I'm a homo'?

Staunch: Why not?

Undercover Brother: Fuck you. My family would kill me if they found out. They're all rugby players, factory workers. Real men.

Staunch: So are we, fool.

Undercover Brother: They don't need to know. What you and me do is nobody else's business.

Staunch: Which is why I'm your fucking 'mate', you chickenshit.

Staunch pushes Undercover Brother.

Undercover Brother: I'll knock you out. And what's wrong with the way we got things here? Why you wanna spoil everything?

Staunch: I've been through all this before. I'm not going to do it again.

I want us to work but if you're too pussy to be honest with yourself—

Undercover Brother: You better not call me that again.

Staunch: Or what? Or what? Pussy.

Undercover Brother: I mean it.

Staunch: Pussy. Pussy, pussy, pussy, pussy. Meow.

Undercover Brother pushes back.

I'm not going to hide in the shadows, James. If you can't sort your shit out, that's it.

Undercover Brother: Are you for real?

Staunch: So what's it gonna be?

Undercover Brother: I can't, man.

Staunch: Then get the fuck out of my house.

Undercover Brother: Are you for real?

Staunch: I mean it.

Undercover Brother hesitates before he exits.

Undercover Brother: I fucking love you, bro.

Staunch: What did you say?

Undercover Brother: Fuck up.

He exits.

*

Christian: Hi, God. It's me again.

But you knew that, right, God?

Well, it looks like Letitia was wrong.

I guess you really can't pray the gay away.

'Cause I've been praying pretty hard, God, but I'm still pretty gay.

I'm tired, God

I'm tired of the way my dad looks at me.

I'm tired of being called a black faggot.

I'm tired of people talking behind my back.

Enough is enough, God.

Enough is enough.

*

Darkness. Moaning. Lights up to reveal Mama Letti plucking out hairs from her chin.

Undercover Brother: Mum?

Mama Letti: How's my beautiful boy?

Undercover Brother: You know how I got this mate? This mate who I've been hanging out with? I gotta tell you something.

Mama Letti: Are you in trouble, son? Are you in trouble with the police? Did you get arrested? Were you drunk driving? Did you run somebody over? Did you get a girl pregnant? Is she Samoan? Is she palagi. Is she Māori. James—is she a Tongan?

Undercover Brother: Nah, it's nothing like that. See, I really like this guy, Mum.

Mama Letti: That's nice.

Undercover Brother: Like, really like him.

Mama Letti: Good. A best friend.

Undercover Brother: *Like* him, like him.

Mama Letti: A best best friend. BFF.

Undercover Brother: Like, a girlfriend.

Mama Letti: O lea?

Undercover Brother: Except he's my boyfriend.

Mama Letti: Wait, what?

Undercover Brother: I'm sort of going out with him.

Mama Letti: Going where? Overseas?

Undercover Brother: I'm kind of gay, Mum.

Mama Letti: Kind of?

Undercover Brother: Well, no. I am gay.

Mama Letti: Are you sure? How do you know?

Undercover Brother: I know, Mum. I've always known.

Mama Letti: What did I do wrong?

Undercover Brother: Nothing, Mum. I've always been like this. It's just the way I am. I never liked girls. Not like this.

Mama Letti: You know what it says in the Bible, James. Maybe we should talk to the minister.

Undercover Brother: I don't need to talk to the minister, Mum. There's nothing wrong with me. I'm just gay, that's all.

Mama Letti: Well, we better buy a pig. For your father. Before you break his heart. Now go and tell your brother. He's smashing weights in the garage.

*

Bro: So what is this big news you have to tell us? Spit it out, I haven't got all day. You're what? You're gay?

Silence. Then Bro laughs. Then laughs again.

What? You think I'm deaf, dumb and blind? What gave it away? Sole. Please. Where do I begin? Your Sonny Bill Williams poster on the ceiling? Your Katy Perry CDs? Who else knows? Let me see. Auntie Carol. Uncle Sefa. Pastor Leifi. The butcher. All the checkout girls at Pak'nSave. We had a pool on when you'd come out, and you just lost me ten bucks, dumbass. I said the end of never! So what are you? A top or a bottom or vers? I bet you're a bottom. I'm a fluent gay speaker now. Since when? Since we tried to find you on Grindr. Me. And cousin Donna. Come on, man, all that time you spend on your mobile, 'surfing'. And then that innocent little 'Oh, I'm just popping out to the shops'. Yeah, we all knew you were hooking up. Man, your profile was funny. Seven inches? More like seven millimetres. Bro. It's all good. We still love you, you big black faggot. And if anyone gives you shit, I'll smash them.

*

Mama Letti: Yeah, okay, my son is a gay. Do you hear me? My son is a FAGGOT! A fa'afāfine. A fakaleiti. He's a homo. Whatever you want to call him. Alright? And I don't care who knows. What the hell are you laughing about, Pesetelo Faumauina? Can you spell child support? 'Cause you sure as hell can't pay it, uh? And what are you shaking your head for, Mele Vaele? Everyone knows you playing more than housie with Mr Afeaki. Yeah, that's right. All the sixes, sixty-six. That boy is my son and I love him. How could I not love my son? He is my flesh and blood. But I think, Oh my boy, my beautiful boy. I get scared for my boy. Scared he is going to go to hell because that's what they say in the Bible, uh? And I don't want my beautiful boy to go to hell. So I pray to God and say, God: Please don't send my son to hell just because he is gay. I don't think he will.

*

Staunch is on the phone.

Undercover Brother walks past. Staunch wolf-whistles at him.

Now that that marriage bill got through—now that enough 'mantally sick' MPs supported it? You know what I'm gonna do? I reckon I'm gonna ask James to marry me one day. Straight up. He's the one sole. We're off to the gym now. Gotta do our reps. Legs tonight. And then we're off to Pak'nSave. Exciting, huh? Then gotta get the place ready for somebody's in-laws. So much for destroying the fabric of society, eh? Yeah, they're cool. They're just happy he's happy. Am I happy? Yeah, I'm happy. Couldn't be happier.

He hangs up. The phone goes. It's for Undercover Brother. Staunch hands the phone over.

Undercover Brother: Sup, Christian? Long time, no see. How you doin', little cousin? What's the matter? Who's giving you a hard time? You tell me who they are and I will fuck them up. Shhh shhhh shhhh. Christian? Lis— lis—no, calm down. Christian, listen to me, okay? It gets better. I promise.

The End

At the Wake

At the Wake started out as a stalled short story about a white grandmother appalled that her *afakasi* grandson would wear an 'ie faitaga to his mother's funeral.

It started to take shape as a play when I added the grandson's father to the mix after asking myself: what if I were in the same room as my Scottish grandmother and my Samoan father, since we never were in life.

But the thing that really brought *At the Wake* to life was a darling woman by the name of Joan Livingstone.

Ours was an unlikely friendship. There I was, a big burly Samoan; there she was, an elderly little British woman from the Wirral who didn't even come up to my shoulder. But it was a friendship that worked—she was the one friend of mine with whom I felt free to discuss anything, and I mean absolutely anything. Nothing was off-limits with Mother Time.

We met in the early 2000s through Joan's late daughter, Lydia. Lydia was producing a play written by a mutual friend. I remember eating pizza with Lydia and the cast in Joan's small art-filled flat on Franklin Road, in Auckland. Even though she was surrounded by one or two larger-than-life actor types, that little silver-haired lady quietly made a strong impression on me as someone who had been around the block once or twice and who possessed a terrific and often wicked sense of humour; someone who was sharp as a tack and incredibly perceptive; someone who was kind and generous.

I got to know her story and she got to know mine. Eventually Joan became my self-professed Auckland nanny. One mistake I made with my own Nan was that I underestimated her, failed to recognise that she'd lived a life and knew the score. I didn't make the same mistake with Joan.

Joan became the chief inspiration for the character Joan in *At the Wake* (although I hasten to add that Joan the character is far more caustic than Joan ever was in life).

I saw Joan the day before she died. She rattled off a litany of agonies ranging from physical pain to emotional anguish. I smiled at Joan and said, 'Oh, how I've missed your whingeing.' She threw back her silver-haired head and laughed.

She will be missed but her spirit lives on in *At the Wake*.

—Victor Rodger

I first encountered Victor Rodger when I was offered the role of Joan in *At the Wake* for a production in Auckland in late 2104. The raw emotional power of Victor's writing combined with his elegant wit won my heart and I immediately agreed to do it. Playing Joan was a breathless, heady rollercoaster ride as the character veers recklessly from deliciously vicious humour and brutal honesty to heartbreaking revelation.

I left New Zealand in 1966 to study acting on a grant from the New Zealand government, and have had a successful international career. Because of my familiarity with the plays of Shakespeare and the ancient Greeks, what resonated most with me about Victor's writing was the depth of honesty in the human relationships he explores and his linguistic skill in the expression of those complex relationships. The critical acclaim for *At the Wake*, and its success with audiences who were moved to laughter and tears simultaneously, was the final proof that Victor's writing touches the heart profoundly—the mark of a great playwright.

—Lisa Harrow, ONZM

For Nora Rodger and Joan Livingstone

At the Wake premiered in 2012 at Centrepoint Theatre in Palmerston North. It was produced by Centrepoint Theatre with the following cast and production team:

Joan	Lynda Milligan
Robert	Samson Chan-Boon
Tofi	Iaheto Ah Hi

Director	Roy Ward
Set Designer	Sean Coyle
Lighting Designer	Phillip Dexter
Costume Designer	Sara Taylor

At the Wake

Characters:

Joan: White.

Robert: Joan's half-Samoan grandson.

Tofi: Robert's Samoan father.

Scene 1

At Joan's apartment.

Darkness. Classical music plays (Mahler). Lights up on:

Joan, a chic elderly white woman, dressed in black, smoking.

The set is empty except for a table, a chair, a hat and a bottle of Johnnie Walker Blue Label.

Joan seems consumed with grief until she notices something out the window.

Joan: That bastard dog's shit on the front lawn again. I swear to God if I ever catch it I'm going to tie a turd around its bloody neck. No, actually, you know what I'm going to do? I'm going to find its owner and throw the turd on *their* front lawn, see how they like it. Someone's obviously trained their dog to shit on mine. I bet it's that dreadful South African woman up at number forty-two, the one who organises the Christmas lights. Did I tell you about her? Turned

51

up outside my front door with some hideous lights. (*in a South African accent*) 'Listen, Joan, you're the only one in the entire street who's resisting this.' Of *course* she's South African. Bloody rock spider. I guess I'm lucky I'm not black or she probably would have shot me. Kept going on and on. Honestly, I thought I was going to have to call the police. Such rage. 'But, Joan, everyone else on the street is putting lights up. Everyone. This is not acceptable. This is not fair.' 'Fair?' I said. 'Neither was apartheid.' And then I told her that I wasn't going to put any lights up outside my own house and that she could take her lights and shove them up her fucking fanny.

Robert:	(*offstage*) Those were your exact words?
Joan:	What do you think?
Robert:	Yes?
Joan:	Good boy. You know your nanny.
Robert:	Oh, yes.
Joan:	I bet it *is* her.
Robert:	If that is indeed what you said then, yes, I'd have to say there's a pretty good chance it is.
Joan:	Go scoop it up for me, will you, kid?
Robert:	What? The turd?
Joan:	I'll just throw it out the window onto her lawn as we drive past. Would that be alright?
Robert:	You're not serious?
Joan:	I'll get a plastic bag, you can put it in there.
Robert:	No.
Joan:	So you would rather let your own grandmother of three score and ten, with her chronic arthritis, her bad back, her gammy knee—you would rather let her

bend down and scoop up that turd herself?

Robert: Stop acting. And since when are you only seventy?

Joan: I don't know what you're talking about.

Robert: More like eighty. And you are not going to guilt me into picking up that dogshit. Sorry.

Joan: Fine. I shall do it myself.

Beat.

I mean it.

Beat.

Right, then.

Joan opens and shuts the front door but stays inside.

Beat.

Robert: I know you're still there.

Joan: Did you hear me?

Robert: I can tell when you're acting.

Joan: How?

Robert: You get this thing in your voice that sounds like you're being, like, y'know—*really* sincere. Only you're not. You're acting.

Joan: Your grandfather could never tell the difference. Especially in bed. 'Did you really enjoy that, Joanie?'

Robert: God, Nanny . . .

Joan: 'Yes, Douglas, yes, it was amazing. The best ever, etc., etc.'

'Really? Or are you acting?' Poor thing. I was always acting. He was hopeless in bed. Hopeless.

Robert: That's nice.

Joan: What are you doing in there? Oh, and he kissed like

a fish gasping for air. I could never tell him, though.
Didn't want to hurt his feelings. The things you
do for love, eh? And at the end of the day he was a
trooper, your grandfather. I'll give him that.

Robert: In what way?

Joan: I know you may find it hard to believe but not every
man could put up with my . . .

Robert: Your unique charms?

Joan: Arsehole. You wouldn't really remember him, would
you?

Robert: Not really.

Joan: He was a lovely man. A good man. But difficult. That
was my nickname for him.

Robert: 'Difficult?'

Joan: 'Oh, Difficult,' I'd say. 'What now?'

Robert: Wow, that's intense.

Joan: He didn't mind me calling him that, if that's what
you're worried about.

Robert: Are you sure about that?

Joan: Would you like to know what I called Jeffrey
Fontaine? I called him 'Delightful'.

Robert: Who is Jeffrey Fontaine?

Joan: I never told you about Jeffrey Fontaine?

Robert: I think I'd remember if you had, with a name like
that. Was he an actor, by any chance?

Joan: Fabulous. Fabulous actor. He played Hamlet to my
Gertrude, even though I was far, far too young to be
playing his mother. Ridiculous casting.

Robert: So did you . . . ?

Joan:	Did we fuck?
Robert:	I was going to say 'Did you have an affair?', actually.
Joan:	Your generation—such delicate creatures. Really, I mean—what? You don't think old codgers like me used to fuck, be sexual beasts like you and your generation?
Robert:	Oh, I know you did because you bloody keep telling me. It's just—there are things. Things a grandson really doesn't need to know.
Joan:	Well, I do beg your pardon, Mary Poppins.
Robert:	Piss off.
Joan:	That's the spirit, kid. And speaking of spirits . . .
Robert:	Get away from that whiskey.
Joan:	How do you know I'm anywhere near it?
Robert:	Because I know you.
Joan:	Just one little shot before we go.
Robert:	No.
Joan:	Johnnie Walker Blue Label, eh? How much was that then?
Robert:	Three hundy.

Joan whistles in admiration.

Well . . . it is a special occasion.

Joan:	Yes.
Robert:	I thought we could have it at the . . .
Joan:	At the aftermatch?
Robert:	Yes. At the aftermatch.

Joan looks at her watch.

Joan:	We'll have to leave soon.

She looks distressed.

Joan: What on earth is taking you so long? It's a woman's prerogative to be late. What's your excuse?

Robert: Windsor knot. I can never get it right.

Joan: That's because you never had a father to teach you.

Robert: What was that?

Joan: I said you should get that new boyfriend of yours to teach you.

Robert: Marcus? He can barely tie his own shoelaces, let alone a Windsor.

Joan: This one does have a job, though, doesn't he? Not like that last creature.

Robert: Don't be mean.

Joan: What was his name again?

Robert: You mean Malik?

Joan: Hideous creature.

Robert: He wasn't that bad.

Joan: *Now* who's acting?

Robert: Marcus is nothing like Malik. He's really lovely and yes, he does have a job. He's a secretary.

Joan: A secretary? And how old is this Marcus?

Robert: Forty-two.

Joan: A forty-two-year-old secretary? Very promising.

Robert: Snob.

Joan: A snob? Moi? Fine. Come on. Come here. I'll do your tie for you.

          Robert enters, a handsome half-Samoan man dressed in a shirt, a tie, a jacket and an 'ie faitaga (formal lavalava).

Joan is horrified.

What the hell are you wearing?

Robert:	Nan—
Joan:	You are not wearing that.
Robert:	Yes. I am.
Joan:	You are not wearing a skirt to your mother's funeral.
Robert:	It's not a skirt. It's an 'ie faitaga.
Joan:	I don't give a shit what it is. You go to your room right now and you change into something more appropriate.
Robert:	I'm not a child, Nan. This is what I'm wearing. Handle it.
Joan:	You can handle my hand on your backside in a minute. Is this how you swan around in New York, is it? I do not understand this.
Robert:	You don't have to.
Joan:	You're not even a real—
Robert:	Don't say it.
Joan:	But you're not. Chief Fuckitty-fuckface was never around, you haven't grown up with the culture . . .
Robert:	I'm not discussing this.
Joan:	For you to do this, to wear that, it's like a slap in the face.
Robert:	For who?
Joan:	Your mother.
Robert:	I'm doing this for her. She's why I'm wearing it. As a tribute.
Joan:	Are you high on drugs? *This* is a tribute to her?
Robert:	Yes.

Joan: This isn't a tribute, Robert. This is a statement. A statement of misguided loyalties to a man and a culture that never did anything for you or your mother. Did that man wipe your bum and change your nappies? No. Did he ever give you a cent? No. Did he even give you so much as a hug? No. Because he took off like Jesse Owens at a KKK rally when he found out your mother was pregnant.

Robert: This isn't about him, Nan. He probably won't even be there, so I want to wear something that—

Joan: What do you mean 'probably won't even be there'? Why would he be there?

Robert: He might have read the obituary.

Joan: What if he did? He never got off his black backside to do anything for her when she was alive. Why would that change now? I tell you what, if he does come, he'll wish he hadn't. I'll make sure of that.

Robert: You wouldn't.

Joan: Want to bet?

Robert: She loved him, Nan.

Joan: She thought she did.

Robert: He meant something to her.

Joan: She was fifteen, Robert. A child. She didn't know any better.

Robert: She loved him, Nan. This is my way of honoring her love. By representing him.

Joan: Isn't your nose enough?

Robert: I'm wearing it.

Joan: Fine. Two can play at this game.

Nan grabs the Johnnie Walker; opens it.

Robert:	No, wait.
Joan:	Cheers.

Joan takes a swig, chokes and is wracked with a loud, hacking cough.

Robert:	Are you alright?
Joan:	Don't mind me. I'm just about to die. Sorry, that was in very poor taste. Here.

She offers the bottle to Robert.

It's open now. Might as well.

Robert takes a swig.

A beat, where grandmother fondly observes grandson.

Come here.

Joan, with fag in mouth, begins to tie Robert's Windsor.

You know who taught me how to tie a Windsor? Laurence Olivier. And let me tell you, it wasn't around his neck either.

Robert:	Speechless.
Joan:	At least your jacket and your tie are smart.
Robert:	They're Armani.
Joan:	Oh, Armani. Very la-de-da. There. Handsome boy. You look wonderful. Except for that bloody skirt.
Robert:	How many times do I have to tell you? It's not a skirt. It's an 'ie faitaga.
Joan:	'It's not a skirt. It's an ear fai-fungus.'
Robert:	Faitaga. 'Ie faitaga.
Joan:	Fie, fie, fie. A fie on your ear-fai-whatsit.
Robert:	I'm wearing it.
Joan:	Please. Change it. For me. Go on.

Robert: This is what I'm wearing. The. End. Curtain.

Joan: I used to push you around in a huge cardboard box when you were a boy. Damn near broke my back. I used to take you to all those movies in the afternoon while your mother was working. I braved rush-hour traffic to pick you up from school. And this—this is how you repay me?

Robert: Now you're really acting.

Joan: Well, Gary will hate it as much as I do. I suppose that's some consolation.

Joan notices Robert's feet.

Look, if you insist on wearing this hideous ensemble, will you at least cut your toenails? They look like gargoyles' claws.

Robert: Gee, thanks.

Joan: You don't get those monstrosities from my side of the family, that's for sure.

Robert: See? Can't say my father never gave me anything. Have you got clippers?

Joan: Check in the . . . uh . . . you know, in the . . .

Robert: Bathroom?

Joan: That's the one.

Robert moves off.

Robert: (*offstage*) Wow.

Joan: What?

Robert: This is quite an impressive little collection you've got here. Codeine.

Joan: For my back.

Robert: Ooooh, Valium.

Joan: Actually, bring that out will you?

Robert returns with the Valium and the clippers.

Joan pops a Valium.

Joan: You drove me to that.

Robert: I thought you weren't meant to drink when you take Valium.

Joan: Whoopsa-daisy.

Robert is about to do his toenails.

Can you go do that outside please, kid?

Robert: Fine.

Joan: I'm sorry, it just makes me want to vomit.

Robert: I said fine.

Robert heads outside.

Joan: No need to get your knickers in a twist.

Robert: I'm not.

Joan: That petulant whinge. How I've missed it. Oh and while you're there . . .

Robert: I am not scooping up that dog shit so you can throw it on that woman's lawn.

Joan: Actually I was going to ask if you'd put it in her letterbox, Mr Smarty Pants.

Robert: You are not serious.

Joan: I'll do it myself, then.

Robert: You are not to put dog shit in anybody's letterbox, do you hear me?

Joan: Ooooh, listen to you. Fine. I'll just take a softball bat to those hideous lions she has on the top of her gate. I've always wanted to do that. I think people who have crap like that on their properties should be shot. It's so . . . what's the word?

Robert: Do you even have a softball bat?

Joan: Vulgar. Actually, yes, I do. Somewhere. It was Will's.

                Robert returns.

Robert: Are you alright?

Joan: To paraphrase Mr Wilde: to lose one child may be regarded as a misfortune. To lose both looks like carelessness.

                Robert goes to comfort Joan but she turns from him, puts on her hat.

                Hat or no hat? What do you think?

Robert: What are you going for? Gloria Swanson in *Sunset Boulevard*?

Joan: It's a simple question.

Robert: Whatever you feel more comfortable in.

Joan: Useless.

Robert: With all due respect, today isn't about you. It's about Mum.

Joan: I know that. Don't you think I already know that? Just answer the question, will you? Hat—or no hat?

Robert: You know Gary hates your hats, so . . .

Robert/Joan: Hat.

Joan: I wonder what music Gary picked. I shudder to think. It'll be something spectacularly cliché like that—that—that Sarah Brightman song.

Robert: 'Time to Say Goodbye'?

Joan: Or—what's that other one? Um—um— 'Unforgettable'. Something that everybody plays. Your stepfather's never had an original thought in his life. I would have picked something with a bit of bite to it. A bit of meaning. Mozart, maybe. Mahler?

Robert:	He asked me if there was a particular song I wanted played. The only one I could think of was 'I Will Survive'. She loved that one. Didn't really seem appropriate though, somehow.
Joan:	Don't you hate how Gary's organised everything within an inch of its life? I wanted to sing. I offered to sing. Gary wouldn't hear of it. He didn't even ask me if I wanted to speak, arsehole. I offered but he said they'd already sent the programme to the printers. Most people at funerals these days, you can't hear a word they're saying, even with a microphone. They're all so choked up with emotion and they don't understand the first thing about projection. Half the time I want to yell out, 'Speak up, we can't hear you.' But instead everyone just sits there politely even though they can't hear a bloody word old Jenny so-and-so is saying, standing a mile away from the mic. By God, if I got up there they'd hear me, alright. They'd hear how much I loved my Olivia.
Robert:	I'm speaking.
Joan:	Gary asked you? He didn't mention that. Congratulations.
Robert:	Please. It's not like I've won an Oscar.
Joan:	Don't be ridiculous. I'm happy for you. Really.
Robert:	I'm not looking forward to it. I'm not like you. I don't like speaking in front of people. Never have.
Joan:	I'll do it for you, if you like. I'm more than happy to. And we won't tell Gary, so it can be a surprise.
Robert:	It's alright.
Joan:	Are you sure? You're absolutely certain?
Robert:	I'm going to do it. For Mum. I have to.
Joan:	Well, kid, if you get choked up and you start to blubber, you just remember to breathe. Alright? You

put your hand on your stomach and you breathe. That way you can talk through your tears. Like this.

Joan pretends to cry.

'I loved you, Olivia.' See? See how I could talk through the tears just then? But if it all gets a bit much, if you can't go on—you just remember that I'm there and you look at me, okay, kid? You just look at my face.

Joan pulls a funny face.

Robert:	Thank you.
Joan:	See? I'm not completely useless. The old do have the odd thing to teach the young. Even now.

Robert looks at his watch.

Do you know many of your mother's friends?

Robert:	I did. There's her neighbour, Ang. She'll be there.
Joan:	That tub-a-rello from the two-storey place?
Robert:	Be nice. Gary said she was really good to mum. Apparently she cooked her heaps of stuff.
Joan:	I'm surprised she didn't eat it all herself.
Robert:	You know sometimes you are very ungenerous, Joan.
Joan:	Oh, Joan now, is it? I must be in trouble. Naughty me.
Robert:	Ang was good to her.
Joan:	I took food round too, you know.
Robert:	I heard.
Joan:	If I could have swapped places with my baby girl . . . to see her suffer like that . . .
Robert:	I know.
Joan:	How are we going to get through this?

Robert:	You've done it before. You tell me.
Joan:	You just do. Life goes on. Whether you want it to or not, it goes on.
Robert:	It's weird, isn't it? When Gary rang to tell me, I was in Central Park. There was this couple under a tree. Crying with laughter. No idea I'd just received the worst news of my life. I mean how could they, but even so . . .
Joan:	The whole business—it's wretched. Wretched, wretched, wretched.

Robert looks at his watch. Joan tries to cover her distress.

	Have you ever been picked up at a funeral?
Robert:	What the hell?
Joan:	Maybe we'll get lucky.
Robert:	Fingers crossed.
Joan:	It was at a service for Eric Wassermayer. He was a big director back in the day. I sat next to his cousin Alec, who'd come over from Berlin. Ach, mein Gott. He came and sat down next to me. The thighs on him. He was some sort of mountain climber. Or was it a goat herder? Something outsdoorsy. Anyway, he pressed his gigantic German thigh against mine and that's all she wrote, folks. The electricity, I tell you. He really got me going.
Robert:	You can stop now.
Joan:	Anyway, we just sat there, side by side. And when the service was over neither of us moved. I suppose people thought we were overcome with emotion. Which we were. Just not the emotion they assumed we were overcome by.
Robert:	You'll notice I haven't asked what happened next. Because I don't want to know.

Joan:	He got up. Looked at me.
Robert:	Bloody hell . . .
Joan:	I followed him into the room where they prepare the bodies. We fucked on the slab. Beat that. Go on. You can't, can you? Can you?
Robert:	I wasn't aware this was a competition.
Joan:	I win, then.
Robert:	Fine. It was an AIDS memorial for my friend Jay. This man, I'd clocked him when I arrived. Bit of a silver fox. A bit George Clooney.
Joan:	Oh, I love George Clooney.
Robert:	Nice body, looked like he worked out.
Joan:	What was his name?
Robert:	We didn't get that far.
Joan:	Slut.
Robert:	He followed me into the toilet. And we . . . got to know each other.
Joan:	So you two had a conversation in the toilet?
Robert:	Yes. With our penises.
	Joan shrieks.
	Until the dead guy's mother opened the door.
Joan:	Oh, darling, you must always lock the doors. Didn't your mother ever teach you that?
Robert:	'What are you doing?'
Joan:	What did it look like?
Robert:	'Show some respect.' God, I felt dreadful.
Joan:	I bet. It's exhilarating isn't it?
Robert:	No, I really felt dreadful. There I was, supposedly

paying tribute to my friend, and his mother walks in on me getting my (*whistles*) you-know-what by a complete stranger.

Joan: What do you think your friend would have said?

Robert: I think—I think he would have laughed.

Joan: There you go then.

Beat.

Joan: Alec Wassermeyer . . . That man had a cock on him like a . . .

Robert: Please, God, no . . . .

Joan: I was at New World the other day and I saw this salami that reminded me of him. I couldn't walk properly for days.

Robert: You are actually making me physically sick.

Joan: Oh, you poor delicate wee thing. Come on, isn't this how you talk to all your gay chums?

Robert: Nanny, I don't talk to *anyone* like this.

Joan: This new conservatism amongst you lot, it's revolting. Babies. Marriage. Mortgages. Why would you want any of that bourgeois rubbish? If I were a gay man I wouldn't want a bar of it. I would just like to be free.

Robert: You're not now?

Joan: Especially not now. I hate getting old. It's shit. You ache. You get bingo wings. See? Bingo wings! And your memory . . . Oh darling, it's so good to have you here. Now I can moan away to my heart's content. I've missed you.

They embrace.

Joan: Funerals are so bittersweet like that. Reuniting people in the most hideous of circumstances.

Robert looks a little uneasy. He checks his watch.

Robert: Right. We better go.

Joan doesn't move.

Joan: You're really going to wear that?

Robert: We've been through this.

Joan: It's insulting.

Robert: I'm sorry you feel that way. We need to go.

Joan: I'm not going anywhere with you unless you get changed.

Robert: Fine. Get a taxi.

Joan: Do you know how much that would cost?

Robert: Ring Gary, then.

Joan: You wouldn't do that to your own grandmother.

Robert: It's up to you. I'm leaving.

Robert grabs the whiskey and exits.

Joan: Excuse me, it's my car, buster.

Beat.

Joan: Robert English, don't you walk away from me like that. Robert?

Beat.

Joan: Oooooh, you little—

The sound of a car horn.

Alright, alright. Keep your skirt on.

Scene 2

At the funeral.

'Time To Say Goodbye' plays as Joan and Robert enter the funeral home.

Joan: I told you, didn't I? Sarah bloody Brightman? Oh God, look at Gary. He's lip-synching.

Robert: He looks sad.

Joan: Yeah. Because now that lazy bastard's going to have to cook for himself.

Robert: I think he heard you.

Joan: Good. (*Joan nods at Gary*) Gary.

          Joan winces as they watch a montage of Olivia's photos.

          That is a *dreadful* photo of me. That's when I put all that weight on after I had my hip done. I bet Gary chose that one on purpose.

Robert: It's a nice one of Mum.

Joan: Aw, look at her in the paddling pool. She was about three, then. That's when we were all on holiday in Hamilton.

          Another photo appears.

          She was pregnant with you in that one.

Robert: Really? Did she know?

Joan: Why do you think she's still smiling? I'm joking.

          Someone offstage shushes Joan.

          Excuse me, did you just tell me to be quiet? At my own daughter's funeral? Yes, that's right. *I'm* the mother. So *you* be quiet.

Robert: That was Ang.

Joan: What?

Robert: That was her friend, Ang.

Joan: Tub-a-rello.

The music finishes.

Celebrant: (*voiceover*) I think you will all agree with me, that was a beautiful and moving tribute to Olivia.

Joan: Where did he find this celebrant? A voice like wilted lettuce and a face only a mother could love.

Celebrant: (*voiceover*) And now we will hear from Olivia's eldest child, Robert, who has flown in from New York. Robert?

Joan: Remember, kid, if you start to blubber, just keep breathing. I'm right here if you need me. Okay? You'll be fine.

Robert takes to the pulpit and looks out over the crowd.

Robert: When I was on the plane, flying here, I kept trying to think about what I wanted to say today.

Joan: (*mouthing*) Louder.

Robert: My mother was—

Joan: (*mouthing*) Bit louder.

Robert: My mother was everything to me.

Joan: Good boy.

Robert: Olivia.

The great and wondrous O.

It was hard. Trying to find the right words to describe how much she meant to me.

How much I loved her. How loved she made me feel.

But no matter what I wrote or read, nothing really conveyed what I felt—feel.

It's weird. You never think about your mum not

being there. At least I never did. Not even when she got sick. I just thought, She'll get through this because she has to. She's my mum. She has to be alright. But now she's gone and . . .

The last time I spoke to her was on Skype last week. She was never that good with technology and she kept pressing the wrong button so that either I could see her but not hear her or I could hear her but not see her and I got so frustrated I yelled at her.

But she just laughed. Which made me laugh.

That's one thing I'm going to miss about Mum. She always used to make me laugh.

Robert looks at the casket.

I can't imagine life without you, Mum.

Robert bites back tears.

Joan: Just breathe, kid.

Robert: Sorry. I don't know if I can do this.

Joan: Yes, you can, kid. Just breathe. You can do it.

Robert: In the end I found this poem. It's only short but in a funny way it comes the closest out of everything I read to summing up how I feel.

A man in an 'ie faitaga enters—Robert's father, Tofi—as Robert begins to read the first three lines of Stevie Smith's poem 'Human Affection'.

When Robert sees Tofi he momentarily stops before finishing the final line.

Robert leaves the pulpit and heads towards Tofi.

Joan sees Tofi.

Joan: Mother. Fucker. Security. Is there security in here? That man there, the one in the skirt . . .

Robert: It's not a skirt.

Joan: That man has not been invited to this funeral. He is not welcome here. (*to Tofi*) How dare you come here today. How dare you.

Robert faces Tofi with an inscrutable expression. Is he going to hit him or hug him?

Robert? What are you doing? Robert?

Tofi opens his arms to Robert.

Tofi: Lopaki?

Robert hesitates for a beat then falls into his father's arms.

They embrace.

Joan: Jesus fucking Christ.

Joan takes in the shocked mourners.

I do beg your pardon.

Scene 3

At the gravesite.

Joan: Thank you, Gary, for allowing me this opportunity to say a few words. I know I speak for all of us when I say what a wonderful tribute you organised for Olivia today. I don't think there was a dry eye in the house when 'Time to Say Goodbye' came on. It was such a beautiful, fitting choice of music. So thank you, Gary.

Most of you will know that I am Olivia's mother, Joan, and that I am an actress. And as an actress I am used to using other people's words. Today is no different. And today, before this grave wherein lies my only daughter, I should like to quote . . . Agatha Christie.

'A mother's love for her child is like nothing else in the world. It knows no law, no pity. It dares all things and crushes down remorselessly all that stands in its path.'

Joan glares at Tofi, who stands with Robert.

'It dares all things and crushes down remorselessly all that stands in its path.' I couldn't have put it better myself. That is what it means to be a mother. That is how I was with Olivia and her late brother, Will. My children mean—meant—everything to me. Anything that tried to get in the way of my love for my children I crushed it down, without remorse, without a second thought.

But there was one thing which I could not crush.

Joan glares at Tofi again.

And that was the cancer that took my darling Olivia with such cruel, but in some ways merciful, swiftness. You faced death with such grace and courage, my darling. If there is anything we can all be happy about today, it is that you are no longer in pain.

Joan is overcome with emotion . . . Until Tofi begins to softly sing a Samoan funeral song.

Joan swiftly pulls herself together.

Trowel, please.

Robert hands her the trowel.

Robert: Unbelievable.

Joan takes the trowel.

Joan: 'Cowards die many times before their deaths.'

Joan glares at Tofi.

'The valiant never taste death but once.

Of all the wonders that I have yet heard,

It seems to me most strange that men should fear,

Seeing that death, a necessary end.

Will come when it will come.'

I love you, Olivia. With everything.

Joan puts dirt on the coffin. She hands the trowel to Robert.

Robert: Love you, Mum.

Robert puts dirt on the coffin.

Robert goes to hand the trowel to Tofi.

Joan: Don't even think about it.

Robert: Please don't cause another scene.

Joan: *Me?*

Tofi: It's alright, Lopaki.

Tofi begins to move off.

Robert:	You're not going?
Tofi:	I think it's better.
Joan:	Well? Go on, then. Off you go.
Robert:	No, wait.
Tofi:	I don't want to upset your grandmother.
Joan:	It's a bit bloody late for that, sunshine.
Tofi:	I don't want to cause any trouble.
Joan:	What do you think you caused ever since you let my daughter fall in love with you?
Robert:	Nan, stop it.
Joan:	Have you no shame? Oh, that's right. You don't. Or else you wouldn't even be here.
Robert:	I asked him to come.
Joan:	What?
Robert:	It seemed like the right thing to do.
Joan:	Christ Almighty.
Robert:	I rang him before I left New York.
Joan:	How did you even know his number?
Robert:	I looked it up.
Joan:	You knew all along he might turn up?
Robert:	I tried to tell you.
Joan:	You should've tried harder.
Robert:	I knew you'd be like this.
Joan:	So you thought you'd ambush me instead?
Robert:	No, that's not what I—
Joan:	Because that's what it feels like to me, Robert. An ambush.

Robert: I wanted him here, Nan. He meant something to Mum.

Joan: Yes, that's right. A broken heart that never really mended. That's what he meant to her.

Robert: I'm glad he's here. For her sake.

Joan: You're a little shit, you know that? (*to Tofi*) And you're a big shit.

Tofi: I shouldn't have come.

Joan: Damn right, you shouldn't have.

Robert: Stay. Please. Come to the wake.

Joan: You have got to be joking.

Robert: I want him there.

Joan: Why?

Robert: I want both of you there.

Joan: What is this? Some macabre happy-family fantasy? Well, you can forget about that.

Robert: Please, Nan.

Joan: If you really want this—this man to come to the wake, fine. But I can tell you this now, I won't be going. So what's it going to be, kid? Me or Daddy-o?

Robert: Please. Not like this. Not today.

Joan: Well, Robert? Come on, big boy. Make your choice.

Tofi: It's alright, Lopaki. I'll go.

Robert: No. You're coming.

Tofi: Are you sure? Your grandmother seems very—

Robert: We'll see you there.

Joan: Uh-uh. Not me, you won't. No way, José.

Robert: Just give us a minute.

Tofi moves off.

Robert looks at Joan.

Let's go.

Joan: Give me the keys.

Robert: Nan . . .

Joan: Give me the keys. I'm going home. You can walk.

Robert: I'll be in the car.

Robert leaves.

Joan stands by herself for a beat and looks at Olivia's grave.

Joan: Did you see that? In all my years . . .

She is emotional as she tries to quote Twelfth Night.

'Make me a willow cabin at your gate

And call upon my soul with the house

Write loyal cantons of contemned love

And sing them loud even in the dead of . . . in the dead of . . .

She breaks off, emotional.

Robert returns.

Joan glares at him.

He holds out his hand.

Joan hesitates for a beat, then takes Robert's hand.

Scene 4

At the wake.

Tofi sits at a table by himself and looks around the room. He seems to notice something—or someone.

Robert enters with the bottle of Johnnie Walker Blue Label and a plate of savouries.

Tofi: That man over there, he keeps staring at me.

Robert: Which—? Oh. That's Gary. Mum's husband.

Tofi: He looks angry.

Robert: Don't worry about him. I never have.

             Joan enters.

Tofi: What about your grandmother?

Robert: I know how to handle her.

Joan: We'll just see about that, Sonny Jim?

             Tofi stands.

Tofi: Oi. Joan. Hello. It's nice to see you again.

             Beat.

             It's been a while.

             Beat.

             I'm very sorry about Olivia.

             Beat.

Robert: Well. This isn't awkward at all, is it?

             Beat.

             Glasses. How about I go and get us some glasses?
             'Yes, Robert, that sounds like a great idea. Why don't
             you?'

             Robert exits.

Joan pulls out a compact and reapplies her lipstick.

Joan:	Why are you here?
Tofi:	Robert ring me.
Joan:	I know he rang you. But why did you come?
Tofi:	Robert ask me to come. I come.
Joan:	Cut the crap, arsehole. Why now? Why after all these years?
Tofi:	He is my son.
Joan:	Which doesn't seem to have meant a great deal to you before.
Tofi:	And Olivia, she was—
Joan:	Yes? She was what?
Tofi:	Olivia was someone who meant a lot to me.
Joan:	Could've fooled me, buster. Could've fooled her.

Robert returns with three glasses.

Robert:	Who's for a drink?
Joan:	I thought you'd never ask.

Robert pours Joan a drink then begins to pour one for Tofi.

Tofi:	Not for me, thank you. I haven't had a drink for over twenty years. Not since I became a Christian.
Joan:	Since you became a what?
Tofi:	I give my heart to the Lord over twenty years ago.
Joan:	Bloody hell. Next you'll be telling me you've started keeping it in your pants.
Robert:	(*to Joan*) Really?
Joan:	You're not Destiny Church, are you?
Tofi:	Bishop Brian is a fine man.

Joan:	Good God, how could anyone take that man seriously when he has such bad hair?
Tofi:	You go to church, Robert?
Joan:	That'd be the day.
Robert:	(*to Tofi*) Would you like me to get you something else to drink?
Joan:	Let him get it himself. Those legs aren't painted on.
Robert:	Dad, what would you—?
Joan:	'Dad'? 'Dad' now, is it? Do you actually understand what that word means?
Robert:	What would you like? An orange juice? A fizzy?
Joan:	How about a milkshake with a little bit of extra ice cream?
Tofi:	No, thank you. I'm fine.
Joan:	For God's sake, it's a wake. Have a drink. What are you worried about? God's going to smite you with a lightning bolt?
Robert:	You don't have to if you don't want—
Joan:	Have. A. Fucking. Drink.
Tofi:	Just a small one, then.

Robert pours.

A bit more. Maybe just a little bit more. Ia, that's good. Thank you.

Robert gives a glass to Joan and to Tofi.

Robert:	I'd like to propose a—

Joan slugs her drink back.

I was going to propose a toast to Mum.

Joan:	Oh. Sorry. I do beg your pardon.

She holds her glass out. Robert hesitates.

I presume you want me to play nice. Then top me up, kid.

Robert: Do you promise to behave?

Joan: Cwoss my heart.

Robert pours.

Of course, I can't make promises that I won't keep. You'd know all about that, wouldn't you?

Robert: Please, I want this to be—

Joan: Like a scene from *Pollyanna?* Where we all play the Glad Game? Well, I'm afraid the only scene I liked in *Pollyanna* was when Hayley Mills fell out of a tree and became a paraplegic.

Robert: I want this to be nice.

Joan: I hate that word.

Robert: Jesus Christ. Civil, then. Is that better?

Tofi: Please—son—do you mind? Not using the Lord's name in vain?

Robert: Oh. Sorry.

Joan: Blasphemy? You're worried about blasphemy? Oh, brother, you are a real trip, you know that?

Robert: Look—Mum would have liked him being here.

Joan: How do you know that? You don't know that.

Robert: You know she would've. And she would have wanted him treated with respect.

Joan: Your mother was a saint. She would have wanted Hitler treated with respect.

Robert: This is hard enough without you making it more difficult.

Joan: Excuse me, I'm not the one who ambushed my own
grandmother with Chief Fu—

Robert: Don't.

Joan: Fine. I will draw on every ounce of my acting ability
to try and be 'nice' to your—guest. But you must
understand, Robert, some parts—some parts are
beyond even me.

Robert: How about an hour or two of 'Dear Old Nanny'?
Think you could manage that?

Joan: (*in an exaggerated old voice*) 'Dear Old Nanny'. I'll
give it a shot.

               Robert raises his glass.

Robert: A toast: to Mum.

Tofi: To Olivia.

Joan: Olivia.

               *Tofi clinks his glass with Robert's and goes to clink Joan's,
               but she ignores him. They all drink.*

Tofi: Oi. That's good. Easy. Easy to drink.

Joan: It should be. It cost three hundred dollars.

Tofi: Three hundred dollars? Gee whiz.

Joan: 'Gee whiz.'

Robert: Not even thirty seconds.

Tofi: You could feed a whole family for two weeks with
three hundred dollars. Are you a rich man now,
Robert?

Joan: He's not going to give you any money so you can go
and blow it all on KFC, if that's what you're asking.

Robert: Goddamnit, Nan. Give it a rest, will you?

Tofi: Oi, sole. You shouldn't talk to your grandmother like that. You need to treat your elders with respect. My father ever hear me talk to my grandmother like that, he knock the teeth right out of my mouth.

Robert: Sorry.

Tofi: Why you apologise to me, uh?

Robert: Sorry, Nan. I shouldn't have spoken to you like that.

Joan: Why not? That's how we talk, isn't it? It's how we are.

Robert: No. Dad's right.

Joan grabs the Johnnie Walker and tops up her drink.

Joan: The father. The son. The holy spirit. And Dear Old Nanny? Fuck me.

She raises her drink.

She sips.

You can taste the Highlands when you drink this. You really can. (*Joan sings*) 'You take the high road and I'll take the low road, / and I'll be in Scotland afore ye, for me and my true love will never meet again / on the bonny bonny banks of Loch Lomond.'

Robert: Anyone want a savory?

Joan: They look disgusting. I told Gary I knew a good caterer. Wouldn't feed this muck to a dog. (*to Tofi*) Sausage roll?

Tofi: Thank you.

Tofi eats.

Mmmmmm. Delicious.

Joan scoffs.

Are you alright, Joan?

Robert: Don't worry. She's just acting. She does that. Quite a bit.

Tofi: How can you tell when she's acting?

Robert: Years of experience. Trust me.

            Joan looks aghast.

            There. See? Acting.

            Joan looks even more aghast.

            Still acting.

            Joan gives up and just looks disgruntled.

            Not acting.

            Tofi finishes his sausage roll.

            Robert passes Tofi the savouries again.

            Here. Have another one.

Tofi: Ia. Thank you.

            Beat.

            I saw you. On that TV show.

Joan: (*sharp*) Which one?

Robert: Nan.

Joan: (*nice*) Which one, dear? (*to Robert*) Better?

Tofi: I forget the name. You played the mother of a dwarf.

Joan: Little and Long?

Robert: *Little and Large.*

Joan: That's what I said, isn't it?

Robert: You said Little and Long.

Tofi: You were really funny.

Joan: (*sharp*) Yes. I know . . .

            Robert glares.

Tofi: But how come you not on the show anymore?

Joan:	I . . . left.
Tofi:	How come?
Joan:	It was time to leave.
Tofi:	They made you look a lot older than you are, uh?
Joan:	That's because the man playing my son was only six years younger than me. Ridiculous casting. Just like *Hamlet*.
Tofi:	That's what I said to Valerie.
Robert:	That's your wife?
	Tofi nods.
Joan:	Does she know you're here today?
	Beat.
	Didn't think so. What do you think God's going to say about that?
Tofi:	I say to Valerie, They must have made her wear a lot of make-up because Joan, she was always so beautiful.
Joan:	Do you really think flattery is going to help you?
Robert:	Please—he's trying.
Joan:	I've been charmed by the best of them, buster. And at the end of the day all the charm in the world doesn't really mean a thing if you discard someone's daughter like a piece of rubbish and leave her to raise a kid on her own before she's even old enough to vote.
Robert:	Mum would have loved that he came.
Joan:	How do you know that?
Robert:	I know how much Dad meant to her.
Joan:	She actually told you that she wanted him here?
Robert:	It's not something we discussed but—
Joan:	So you don't know, do you?

Robert:	I knew my mother, Joan.
Joan:	What if you're wrong?
Robert:	I'm not.
Joan:	How can you be so sure?
Tofi:	Your grandmother. She's still angry with me.
Joan:	You got that right.
Tofi:	I know what I did was wrong, Joan, but I'm here.
Joan:	So that makes everything alright, then? Wipes the slate clean, does it?
Tofi:	That's not what I mean.
Joan:	Do you have other children?
Tofi:	Three.
Joan:	Any girls?
Tofi:	One.
Joan:	Suppose someone took her innocence. Made her cry herself to sleep while you looked on, utterly helpless. How do you suppose, Mr Christian, how do you suppose that might make you feel?
Tofi:	I suppose it would make me feel very angry.
Joan:	For starters.
Robert:	Look, Nan . . .
Joan:	If you say 'Look, Nan' one more time, I swear to God I'm actually going to give you something to look at.
Tofi:	I'm not that man anymore.
Joan:	How convenient.
Tofi:	I come here today. To say sorry. To Robert. And you. And Olivia.
Joan:	Well guess what? You're too late. And don't you dare

blame that on island time.

Robert: Oh no, you didn't.

Tofi: I know it can't have been easy when I . . .

Joan: Go on, say it.

Tofi: When I . . .

Joan: When you walked out on a pregnant fifteen-year-old? You have no idea.

Robert: Come on, Nan.

Joan: And neither do you.

Robert: What's past is past.

Beat.

Tofi: When Robert rang me I pray to God and I ask him, Lord, what is the right thing to do? And God tell me, Today the boy need his father.

Joan: You needed God to tell you that? Quite frankly, if it took God this long to tell you that Robert needed his father, well, I'm sorry, but he's not much chop really, is he?

Tofi: He tell me the right thing to do is to come to the funeral. To ask forgiveness.

Joan: So *that's* why you came? Because you want something? Now it makes sense.

Robert: That's not what he's saying.

Joan: You're wasting your time. Robert may fall for your little humble pie routine but I've seen it all before. I'll never forgive you for what you did to . . . to . . . to . . . to Olivia. Never. 'I'm sorry?' Talk is cheap, buster. Character is action. You're just full of words, words, meaningless words.

Tofi: I know nothing I do can make up for all the hurt I

caused but if there's anything I could do to make it
better . . .

Joan: Anything? You mean it?

Tofi: Of course.

Joan: Then there is one thing I've always wanted to do.

Robert: What?

Joan stands and walks over to Tofi.

What are you doing?

Joan: You're having your little fantasy, Robert. Now it's my
            turn.

Joan eyeballs Tofi.

Stand up.

Tofi stands up. Joan suddenly slaps his face.

Robert: Oh-em-effing-gee. Did that really just happen?

Tofi: Did that help?

Joan: Actually, no.

Robert: That was mental. Even for you. Everyone's looking
            now.

Joan waves.

Joan: (*nods*) Gary.

Robert: (*to Tofi*) Are you okay?

Tofi: I—I'm fine.

Robert: No more slapping anyone's face, Joan, you hear me?

Robert tops up his father's drink and his own.

Joan: What about me?

Robert: You've had enough.

Tofi drains his glass.

Tofi:	There's another reason why I come. I know the pain of losing a mother. That part of you that can never be replaced. The part of you that is your mother.
Joan:	Give me a break.
Robert:	He's talking about his mother, for God's sake. I mean goodness' sake. Sorry.

Joan dramatically takes a deep, disapproving breath then looks away.

	Your mother—when did she die?
Tofi:	Five years ago.
Joan:	What of? Disappointment?
Tofi:	She have the Alzheimer's.
	Sometimes she used to think I was my father. One time she even think I was her mother. My mother, she die in my arms.
Robert:	In your arms? Wow.
Tofi:	She was like you, Joan.
Joan:	What do you mean?
Tofi:	She was beautiful. Life wasn't always easy for her. But she was strong. Always so strong. Watching her change with the Alzheimer's, it was . . .

Joan stands.

Robert:	Where are you going?
Joan:	I'm going outside. I need a ciggie.
Robert:	They'll kill you, you know.
Joan:	Sometimes I wish they'd bloody hurry up and do the job.
Robert:	You don't mean that?
Joan:	No, kid. Not today.

Joan moves to the smoking area.

Lights down on Robert.

Joan's hand is shaky as she tries to light a cigarette.

Tofi appears.

What the hell do you want? Another slap?

Tofi: Here, let me help you.

Joan: I don't need your help.

But she can't get the lighter going.

Tofi: Let me try? Please.

Joan relents.

Father God, if it is your will, Lord, please let Joan's lighter work. Amene.

Tofi lights the cigarette for Joan.

Ia, there you go. It's a miracle.

Joan blows smoke in his face, which makes him cough.

Tofi can't help laughing.

Ah, Joan. Still the same.

Joan: You're not. You got fat. Positively porky.

Tofi rubs his belly, laughing.

Tofi: Life.

Joan: And lots of it, from the look of you.

Tofi: May I have a sikaleki, please?

Joan: A what?

Tofi: A cigarette.

Joan: Let me guess. You haven't had one of these since you became a Christian either?

Tofi: The doctor say to stop since I have my heart attack.

Joan:	Oh, you have one, do you?
Tofi:	Yes, I have the heart attack in April.
Joan:	No. I meant a heart.
Tofi:	I still have a sikaleki now and then. Don't tell Valerie, uh? She kill me.
Joan:	I must ask Robert for the number. I think we could have a lovely little chat, she and I. 'Hello, Valerie. You don't know me. But I know your husband. Do you?'

Tofi is a bit taken aback.

Joan:	That wiped the smile off your mug, didn't it? This Valerie—where exactly does she think you are today? Church? Down at the TAB? KFC?
Tofi:	She think I'm at work.

Silence.

Joan:	Thou shalt not lie. That's what the Big Man says, isn't it? Naughty you.

Joan tries to ignore Tofi, who waits expectantly.

Fuck, alright—here.

Joan offers Tofi a cigarette.

Tofi:	Uh—your lighter? Fa'amolemole?
Joan:	What next? Parking money?

She hands him the lighter.

Tofi:	Ia, thank you.

Tofi lights up.

This reminds me of those times at your place. When we used to sneak out and have a smoke in the garden. You remember?

Joan:	I don't remember.
Tofi:	I do. Do you remember? I used to watch the way you

smoke and it make me think of a glamour movie star. Like Elizabeth Taylor or . . . ?

Joan: 'Keep your face always toward the sunshine—and shadows will always fall behind you.'

Tofi: Excuse me?

Joan: Walt Whitman. You're a shadow, Tofi. A long, long shadow.

Tofi: Lopaki ask me to come.

Joan: He wouldn't have. If he knew all the trouble you caused.

Tofi: I couldn't say no to my son. Not today.

Joan: And you wouldn't have come if you knew, either.

Tofi: What trouble?

Tofi puts a hand on Joan's arm.

What do you mean?

Joan glares at his hand.

Joan: Don't touch me, Shadow.

Tofi withdraws his hand.

Tofi: Sorry.

Joan: Disappear, Shadow. Go back where you came from. Begone from this place. Please.

Joan exits.

Lights down.

Lights up on Robert, alone, biting his nails.

Joan appears. She looks at him for a beat.

I haven't seen you bite your nails since you were at primary school.

Robert puts his hands down.

Robert:	Got your fix?
Joan:	Had my fill.
Robert:	You alright?
Joan:	Oh, chirpy as a chirpy old box of birds, darling. Chirpy chirp chirp.
Robert:	I see your sarcasm and I raise you my indefatigable optimism.
Joan:	Oh, *Pollyanna* . . .
Robert:	It's going pretty well, don't you think? With Dad. Apart from the slap.
Joan:	Maybe I should have given him a backhand as well. That might have been better.
Robert:	Where is he?
Joan:	Don't know. Don't care.
Robert:	He is still here isn't he?
Joan:	I hope not.
Robert:	Joan, what have you done?
Joan:	Maybe he went to find some Tupperware so he could take home all the leftovers. Not that there'll be any the rate he's going.

Tofi appears.

Robert:	There you are. I was worried.
Tofi:	Why for?
Robert:	I thought Nan might have attacked you again or something.
Tofi:	What I tell you about showing respect, uh?
Robert:	Sorry, Nan.

Tofi checks his watch.

Tofi: Valerie will want to know where I am.

Robert: If you have to go . . .

Joan: Just go.

Robert: It's okay. I understand.

Tofi: I can stay for a little while longer.

               Tofi reaches for the whiskey.

               May I?

Robert: Of course.

               Beat.

               Gary came over when you were having your smoke.

Joan: What did he want?

Robert: He wanted to know who the other guy in the skirt was. 'Should I call the cops, Robert? He didn't try it on Joan, did he?' I sort of explained what happened. That you'd lost your mind.

Joan: Very funny

Robert: You should have seen him. 'Tell your grandmother to pull her head in.'

Joan: Hands on hips, was he?

Robert: 'This is your mother's wake.' Like I needed reminding. 'This is your mother's wake.'

               Why do they call it a wake?

Joan: One last chance for the dead to wake up.

Robert: What?

Joan: In the olden days . . .

Robert: You mean when you were little?

Joan: Cheeky shit. They used to put you on the kitchen table when you popped your clogs. Everyone would gather round, have a drink and a bit of a chin wag.

Robert: For what?

Joan: To make sure the final curtain had actually fallen.

Tofi: Curtains? What?

Joan: Sorry, what? Did somebody say something?

Robert: Nan . . .

Joan: My hearing. It's not what it used to be.

Robert: She means they'd get together and wait to make sure they were really dead.

Tofi: Ah. I see.

Joan: Lead poisoning. People—poor people—they used to get lead poisoning from their cups and plates and drop down dead. Only some of them weren't actually dead, but they'd get buried alive.

Robert: Sucks to be them.

Joan: So people started to gather round. Just to make sure they were dead.

Robert: One last chance for the dead to wake up?

Joan: Exactly.

Robert: Imagine if mum woke up and saw us all together like this. I mean, this is the first time we've all been in the same room together, right?

Joan: And the last.

Robert: I wonder what she'd say.

Tofi: She'd probably drop dead again.

Tofi and Robert laugh. Even Joan can't help laughing.

Robert: Oh my God, he actually made you laugh!

. . . But Robert's laughter soon turns to sobs.

Both Joan and Tofi try to comfort him.

Joan: It's alright, kid.

Tofi: Fa'amalosi, Lopaki.

Robert: She's gone. She's really gone. I can't believe it. I'm never going to hear her voice again. Never going to see her again. I should've been there.

Joan: They gave her a year, kid. Who knew she'd be gone in a month?

Robert: It doesn't matter. I should've been here.

Joan: She knew you loved her, kid, that's all that matters.

Robert: I'm an asshole.

Joan: No—your father's the arsehole.

Robert: Do you know why I didn't come home right away? Because I was hanging out for this big party at Splash.

Tofi: Is that a swimming pool?

Robert: No, it's a nightclub.

Tofi: Why do they call it Splash?

Joan: Do we really want to know?

Robert: It's just a nightclub. A stupid nightclub.

Joan: Don't beat yourself up, kid.

Robert: But if I'd come home then maybe I could have been with her when she died. Like you were. Now I'll never get another chance to tell her how much I loved her.

Joan: She knew, darling. Of course she knew. You were the light of her life, Robert.

Robert: When we die, do you think that's it?

Joan: I like the Bhuddists. Birth. Death. Rebirth. (*to Tofi*)

And if there's any justice in this world, you'll come back as a woman.

Tofi: Reincarnation? Leai, I don't believe in that.

Robert: (*to Tofi*) Where do you think she is?

Tofi: In Heaven. Your mother is in Heaven with the rest of the angels.

Joan: I think I'm going to be sick.

Robert: I don't really believe in Heaven. Or Hell.

Joan: You know what Sartre says, don't you, darling? Hell is other people. And he's right.

Tofi: Well, I do believe in Heaven. And I do believe in Hell. And I know in my heart your mother is up there. Looking down on you right now.

Robert gets emotional.

Robert: Mum . . .

Tofi: It's okay, Lopaki. It's okay. I bet your mother was very proud of you.

Joan: She was.

Tofi: You've grown into a handsome boy. And you wear the 'ie faitaga? Ia, you're a good boy to wear the 'ie faitaga to your mother's funeral, Lopaki.

Robert: I thought it was important.

Tofi: Do you speak Samoan?

Joan: No, he doesn't.

Tofi: Leiloa fa'a Samoa? Oi, kalofa e.

Robert doesn't understand.

But you wear the 'ie faitaga?

Joan: Fie, Fie, Fie.

Tofi: Ia malo, Lopaki. Where you get it?

Robert:	I borrowed it from a mate in New York.
Tofi:	What's his name?
Robert:	Actually I don't really know him. He's more of a mate of a mate. He works for the UN.
Tofi:	So, New York? That's where you live, uh?
Robert:	Two years now.
Tofi:	Oi. And what you do there?
Robert:	I work for MFAT.
Tofi:	The who?
Joan:	MFAT. Fat, fat, fat.
Robert:	Ministry of Foreign Affairs and Trade.
Tofi:	Oi. That sounds very important. You married yet? You got a family?
Robert:	Um . . . no, I'm not married.
Tofi:	You got a girlfriend? Handsome boy like you, I bet all the girls chase after you.
Joan:	How much you want to bet?
Robert:	A girlfriend? No.
Tofi:	Oh, well. You young. Plenty of time for you to find a wife, settle down, uh?
Robert:	Ummm . . . .
Joan:	You're not going to tell dear old Dad here about you-know-who? Since you're having this heartwarming little getting-to-know-you session?
Tofi:	Ah, so there is someone? Someone special?
Joan:	Go on, Robert. Don't be shy.
Robert:	It's nothing, really.
Joan:	I don't think you-know-who would like to be described as 'nothing'.

Robert:	Nan . . .
Joan:	Well, come on, Robert. Tell dear old Daddykins.
Robert:	I don't think this is the time or the place.
Joan:	I think all bets are off today, don't you?
Robert:	Quit it, Joan.
	Beat.
Joan:	Robert lives in New York with his boyfriend, Marcus. Don't you, Robert?
Tofi:	Excuse me? With your what?
Joan:	(*to Robert*) What are you looking at me like that for? I'm just making conversation. Isn't that what you wanted me to do?
Tofi:	Lopaki?
Robert:	I live in New York. With my boyfriend. Marcus.
Tofi:	So you are a gay?
Joan:	Which you would have known if you'd ever kept in touch with your son.
Robert:	Yes, I'm gay.
Tofi:	I see. And your mother—she knew this?
Robert:	She did.
Tofi:	Kalofa e.
Joan:	Well, come on, Mr Christian. Aren't you going to do your whole 'You've got no right to live on God's green Earth' routine?
Tofi:	I don't think Robert needs any lectures today. But you know, Lopaki, homosexuality is a sin in the eyes of God. And this choice to have this lifestyle—this is not a good choice.
Joan:	That sounded a bit like a lecture to me, kid.

Robert:	With all due respect, Tofiala . . .
Joan:	Is it Tofiala? I always thought it was Toffee Pop. Toffee Pop! Toffee Pop!
Robert:	With all due respect, Tofiala, being gay isn't a choice.
Tofi:	Of course it is.
Robert:	No, it . . . No, it isn't. Anyone who actually chose to be gay would have to be out of their minds to put up with all the shit you have to deal with. Especially from the ignorant and the uninformed. You're born gay.

Robert pours himself a drink.

Tofi:	I'm not going to lecture you, Lopaki. But God said it is a sin for a man to lie with a man as he would lie with a woman.
Joan:	Was that 'lie with' or 'lie to'?
Tofi:	He said it is an abomination.
Robert:	Yeah, so I've heard.
Tofi:	Besides, doesn't it hurt?
Robert:	Excuse me?
Tofi:	When the man puts his thing up your . . . ?
Robert:	Oh my God.
Tofi:	Are you the man or the woman?

Joan giggles.

Robert:	You think this is funny?
Joan:	God, yes.
Tofi:	Sodomy is not natural, son. That's why God created Adam and the Eve. Not Adam and the Steve.
Robert:	This is not a conversation I ever imagined having at my mother's wake. But while we're on the topic: not all gay men have . . . .

Tofi: Not all gay men have what?

Robert: Y'know. Sex where they . . . y'know . . . enter and exit.

Joan: Yes. Sometimes they just hold hands and watch Bette Davis movies, don't they, darling?

Robert: Sometimes we just . . . do other stuff that doesn't involve . . . you know . . . like . . . you know . . . ?

Tofi: No. I'm not sure what you mean.

Joan: Ask him what they do at AIDS memorials.

Robert: Thank you, Joan, that's quite enough.

Tofi: Your mother, she must have been disappointed.

Robert: I beg your pardon?

Tofi: If any of my children were gay . . .

Robert: One of your children *is* gay.

Tofi: If any of my other children were gay . . .

Robert: And for the record, my mother was not disappointed. My mother loved me and accepted me for who I am.

Tofi: She was alright with this?

Robert: Well, she might have been a bit surprised.

Joan: I wasn't. Not the way you always made a beeline for your cousin Yasmin's Barbie dolls .

Tofi: Kalofa e. Your mother should have raised you . . .

Robert: Wait, wait, wait, wait, wait. Are you about to criticise my mother? At her wake? I don't think so.

Tofi: But it's true, Lopaki, she should have raised you . . .

Robert: Whatever you're about to say, I don't want to hear it.

Tofi: She should have raised you—

Robert: Let's just drop it, okay?

Tofi:	I will pray for you, Lopaki.
Robert:	For what? God to make me straight?
Tofi:	I don't want you to go to hell, Lopaki. I want you to join your mother in Heaven. 'Do you not know that wrongdoers will not inherit the kingdom of God?'
Joan:	Oh, Christ.
Tofi:	'Do not be deceived. Fornicators, idolaters, adulterers, arsenokoites . . .'
Robert:	Arse-what?
Tofi:	Arsenokoites.
Robert:	What the hell are they?
Tofi:	Sodomites.
Robert:	Oh. You mean butt-fucking arse bandits? Why didn't you just say so?
Tofi:	'. . . arsenokoites, thieves, the greedy, drunkards, revilers, robbers . . .'
Joan:	You're *still* going?
Tofi:	'None of these will inherit the kingdom of God. And this is what some of you used to be. But you were washed, you were sanctified, you were justified in the name of the Lord Jesus Christ and in the Spirit of our God.' There is still time, Lopaki. There is still time for you to choose a better path. To be sanctified.
Joan:	Well, Robert. What do you think about that?
Robert:	You know what?
	He pours himself another drink and has a gulp.
	I think I'd like to know what the Bible says about walking out on a pregnant fifteen-year-old girl. Never seeing your child with her. Never giving her a cent.
Joan:	Me too.

Robert:	Suddenly I forget why I thought inviting you was a good idea.
Joan:	Hear bloody hear.

Robert finishes his drink, then stands and glares at Tofi, looking like he really could hit him.

But instead, he rips off his 'ie faitaga, throws it to the floor, and stands there in his black designer underwear.

	Robert? What are you doing? I can't believe I'm saying this, kid, but I think you should put your skirt back on. Robert? Put the skirt back on and sit down or else Gary really will call the cops.
Robert:	Nan's right. You're an arsehole.

Robert goes to pour another drink.

Joan:	Maybe you should have a break, kid.
Robert:	That's rich.
Tofi:	Lopaki. Listen to your grandmother. Put your 'ie faitaga back on. Lopaki.
Robert:	Don't call me that. My name is Robert. Got it? It's Robert. Robert English. The son of Olivia English. I carry her name. Her name, not yours. Because she raised me. Not you. Where do you get off telling me what to do?

Robert goes to pour, but Tofi stops him.

Tofi:	Awa.
Robert:	You want a go? Huh?
Joan:	Robert, stop it.
Robert:	You want a go? Come on then, old man.

Tofi suddenly grabs hold of Robert's wrist.

Joan:	Don't you hurt him.

Robert struggles but he can't break free.

Tofi:	Put it down.
Robert:	Get your damn hands off of me.
Joan:	Robert . . .
Tofi:	Put it down.

Robert puts the bottle down.

Now put your 'ie faitaga back on.

Robert:	Fuck you.
Joan:	Do as your father says, Robert. Put it on.
Tofi:	You remember where you are. And why you here, uh?
Robert:	Me, remember? I don't care what you say about me, old man. But you don't criticise my mother. Ever. You got that? You don't have the right. You understand? My whole life, she never said a word against you. Even though she had every reason to. You just remember that, okay?
Joan:	Well said, Robert. Well said.
Tofi:	Alright, Lopaki. Robert. I'm sorry.
Robert:	Who the fuck do you think you are? 'Your mother should have raised you' what? 'Your mother should have raised you' what?
Tofi:	Forget about it.
Robert:	Say it. 'Your mother should have raised you' what? Just fucking say it.
Tofi:	Your mother should have raised you . . .
Robert:	Raised me what?
Joan:	You don't need to torture yourself like this, Robert.
Robert:	No, no—dear old Dad was just about to tell me how he thinks Mum should have raised me, which I find rather fascinating, seeing how he never spent a day

helping her raise me. So you were saying, dear old Dad, 'Your mother should have raised me . . .'? Come on. Say it. 'Your mother should have raised me . . .'?

Beat.

Tofi: Your mother should have raised you better.

Robert: Sorry, I didn't quite catch that last word. 'Better', did you say? Lovely. And if she'd raised me better, done a better job—then I wouldn't have turned into such a great big dirty homo? Is that what you're saying?

Tofi: I shouldn't have said anything.

Joan: You shouldn't even be here.

Robert: So I could have been straight instead and knocked someone up and then fucked off like you did?

Joan: Alright, Robert, you've had your fun.

Robert: This is what you wanted isn't it? I thought you'd be happy.

Joan: Time to put your skirt back on and sit down. Alright?

Robert: I'm twenty-five. The same age you were when you took off, right? How can someone even do that? What kind of man does that?

Robert scoops the 'ie faitaga off the floor and looks at it.

What was I thinking?

Robert throws the 'ie faitaga in Tofi's face.

Take it. Take it and get the hell out of here.

Tofi: I know you're upset, Robert, but . . .

Robert: I'm not going to say it again.

Tofi: You must believe me when I say . . .

Robert tries to push Tofi away but Tofi grabs him in a big bear hug.

I am still your father and you are still my son.
Nothing will ever change that, Robert.

Robert: What are you doing? Let go of me. I said let go.

Robert bursts free and glares at Tofi.

Don't you ever touch me again. You understand?

Tofi: I didn't come to upset you, Robert. I came here to
support you. You asked me to come, so I come.

Beat.

Joan: See all the trouble you've caused today, Toffee Pop?
What did you expect? I mean, really, what did you
think coming here would achieve?

Tofi: I come for Robert.

Joan: Cut the bullshit. You came because you wanted
something. A Get Out of Jail Free card for when you
meet Him Upstairs so you don't get cast into the fiery
pits. Nothing like a nasty little brush with mortality
to make you set your affairs in order.

Robert: What?

Joan: He told me he had a heart attack. So he's trying to
put things right. Just in case. Aren't you?

Tofi: My son ask me to come. His mother is dead. I come.

Joan: You can't admit it, even now? But then, telling the
truth was never really your forte, was it? You know
what I think, Toffee Pop? I think it's time for you to
do what you do best. Leave.

Beat.

Tofi: You take care, Robert. You too, Joan. But no matter
what either of you think, I did love Olivia.

Joan: I don't think you have any idea what love means.
Because love sometimes means doing things which
are hard. Tough. Not turning up when it's too bloody

late. Now disappear, Shadow.

She grabs a sausage roll and begins to eat it.

Disappear.

Tofi turns to go.

Robert picks up his 'ie faitaga and looks at it for a beat.

Tofi is almost offstage when . . .

Robert: I wore this for you. In case you didn't make it. Never worn one before.

Beat.

Why? Why did you leave?

Tofi: I was young, Robert.

Joan: You were old enough to know what you were doing.

Tofi: I was stupid.

Robert: That's not a reason.

Beat.

This might be the last time we ever see each other, Tofiala.

Beat.

Tofi: When Olivia tell me she was pregnant—I wasn't ready to be a father.

Robert: That's it?

Tofi: I'm not proud of what I did, Robert. Leaving your mother to raise you by herself.

Joan: They were never by themselves. They always had me.

Robert: You never came back.

Tofi: I thought about it. But the longer I leave it, I think — she wouldn't want to see me. Or you.

Robert: You made her heart sing, Tofi. That's why I rang you.

Because you made her heart sing.

Tofi: She made mine sing too, Robert. But sometimes—
            sometimes things don't work out the way you want
            them to. I think maybe you know that already.

            Tofi turns to go.

Robert: Wait. Stay. Have another drink with a sodomite.

            *Robert begins to put his 'ie faitaga back on. Struggles
            with the straps. Tofi helps him.*

Joan: Why are you letting him get away with it?

Robert: With what?

Joan: With everything.

Robert: Look, let's just have a drink and just sit here with
            each other and try and be normal. Like a normal
            family. A boy sitting with his father and his
            grandmother at his mother's wake. Do you think we
            can just do that for a moment?

            Robert pours drinks for everyone.

            Joan raises her glass.

Joan: Happy families.

            No one clinks glasses.

            I said to Olivia once, I said, How? How do you do it?
            And she said to me, What choice do I have? She said
            it with a smile.

Tofi: That smile . . . .

Robert: How do you do what?

Joan: How do you not hate that man after what happened?

Robert: She wasn't about hate, Nan. She was about love. You
            know that.

Joan: Yes, she was. But that capacity for love, for

forgiveness—I have no idea where she got it from. It didn't come from me, that's for sure.

Joan: I couldn't have done what she did. Wouldn't. Won't.

Robert: That's what I never understood. She's the one he left. If anyone had a reason to hate Dad, it's her. Not you.

Joan: Perhaps if you had children you'd understand, Robert.

Tofi's phone rings. He checks the caller ID. He hesitates for a beat before he answers, moving away from the table.

Tofi: (*on phone*) Malo, Valerie.

Joan raises her glass.

Joan: Oh, hi ya, Val! (*singing*) Val-der-i, Val-der-a, Val-der-i, Val-der-a-ha-ha-ha-ha-ha—

Tofi: (*on phone*) Oh, that's an old friend.

Joan: Yes, Toffee Pop is my bestest fwend in the whole wide world. (*singing*) Val-der-i, Val-der-a . . .

Robert: Stop it. That's enough.

Tofi: (*on phone*) She just ask me if I want a Toffee Pop.

Joan: 'Cause he already shovelled all the sausage rolls down his cakehole.

Robert: For God's sake.

Tofi: (*on phone*) Uh, we're at a . . . at a, uh . . . party.

Joan: (*singing*) 'Knees up Mother Brown, / Knees up Mother Brown, / Knees up, knees up, / Never let the breeze up, / Knees up Mother Brown.'

Tofi: (*on phone*) Ia, I'll be home soon.

Joan: (*terse*) Not soon enough.

Tofi: (*terse*) I'll be home when I'm home.

Joan: Ooooh, someone's got their panties in a bunch.

Tofi: I have to go.

Joan: He had a ciggie and a drink, Val! Isn't he a naughty
            boy?

Tofi: Ia, fa.

Joan: Toodle-oo!

            Tofi hangs up.

            Robert looks at Joan.

            What?

Robert: Did you hate Tofi right from the start?

Tofi: No, she didn't. Your grandmother, she used to be very
            kind to me.

Robert: She did?

Tofi: Very kind.

            Tofi and Joan exchange a look.

Joan: That was a long time ago.

Tofi: I meet Joan when I first get to New Zealand and get a
            gardening job.

Robert: You hired Dad to do your garden?

Joan: Douglas hired him. As a surprise. Poor old Difficult
            Douglas. It was just after Will had died. Things were
            rather fraught. Trimming the hedges wasn't exactly
            high on my agenda.

Tofi: The garden—it was crazy. Wild. Weeds everywhere.

Joan: Douglas probably thought a nicely trimmed hedge
            would be the solution to everything. Oh, Difficult,
            how wrong could you be?

Tofi: New city. New language. New people. It was all very
            different for me but your grandmother, she make me

feel very welcome. She used to bring me crumpets.
I never have crumpets before. I always like saying
that word: Thank you for the crumpets, Joan. Such a
funny word. Crumpet.

Robert: So you didn't always hate him?

Tofi: No. Not always.

Joan reaches for the bottle, pours a shot, sculls it.

Joan: Don't you dare say another word or God help me I'll
break your skull open with that bottle.

Robert: Nan.

Tofi: Today he deserves the truth.

Joan: I mean it.

Robert: What is he talking about?

Joan: It doesn't matter.

Tofi: We're being honest with each other now. Isn't it time
you were too?

Joan: Don't listen to him, kid. He's drunk.

Robert: No, wait. What does he mean? Honest about what?

Tofi: About . . .

Joan: You come here today. You ruin Olivia's funeral with
your little stunt, you stir everything up again after
all these years and now you have the audacity to sit
there, when your own wife doesn't even know you're
here and tell me that it's time to tell the truth?

Robert: The truth about what?

Joan: I said it doesn't matter. Not a word.

Tofi: I work hard on that garden. My first job in New
Zealand, I want to do a good job. I want to impress
Joan and Douglas. And Joan, she start to watch me.

Joan: I meant what I said before, Shadow.

Joan grabs the bottle, but Robert snatches it off her.

Robert: What do you mean 'watch you'?

Tofi: Like watch me. While I work. And I think to myself, Why is she watching me? She not trust me to do a good job? But she can see for herself I do a good job. So why she watching me?

Robert: Wait, wait, wait—what were you wearing?

Tofi: A pair of Stubbies.

Robert: And what else?

Tofi: Nothing. It was hot. The middle of summer.

Robert: So you're there. In your Stubbies. Nan is watching you and then?

Tofi: And then one day she say, 'Tofi. It's so hot. Why don't you come inside and have a break.' And so I go inside and have a break. And then . . .

Silence.

Robert suddenly clicks.

Robert: Oh-em-effing-gee.

Joan: Robert . . .

Robert: You Alec Wassermeyer-ed him? Oh, my life. You did, didn't you?

Joan: Robert, wait. I can explain.

Robert: You and him? Wow.

Robert shudders.

Images. In my head.

Joan: It didn't mean anything.

Robert: Out, out. Get out.

Joan:	It was a dalliance.
Robert:	Yuck.
Joan:	An insignificant little dalliance.
Robert:	Now who's being delicate? You mean you fucked my father?
Tofi:	You watch your mouth.
Joan:	It was a fling. A stupid meaningless fling. Will had just died. Douglas and I were barely talking. Grief does strange things to people, you know?
Robert:	Like make them fuck the gardener?
Tofi:	Se, Robert, sōia!
Robert:	'Here's to you, Mrs Robinson.'
Joan:	Your father helped me forget. For a moment or two he helped me forget the pain. He helped me forget Will.
Tofi:	Your grandmother, she wasn't the only one who was sad.
Robert:	Mum?
Tofi:	Sometimes she come to talk to me, about her brother. How she missed him.
Joan:	I could see Olivia had a crush on him. So could Douglas. 'Our little girl's growing up.' He thought it was a huge joke.
Robert:	And you? What did you think?
Joan:	She was still a child, Robert. I never thought it would go beyond a silly schoolgirl crush.
Robert:	Never wanted it to either, I bet.
Joan:	Don't be so disgusting.
Robert:	I bet you were jealous, weren't you?

Joan:	I'm not the villain of this piece, Robert. The villain sits right beside you.
Robert:	And the Oscar goes to . . .
Joan:	Alright, yes. Maybe I was jealous. Because I could tell your father liked her too.
Tofi:	I loved her.
Robert:	So that's what this has been about? All this time? That's why you've hated him? Because he went off with Mum? You're unbelievable.
Joan:	That is the most hurtful thing you could ever say to me.
Robert:	Now it all makes sense. Why you never wanted me to see him.
Joan:	Well, I'm sorry, Robert, but let's be honest, he wasn't exactly banging down the door to try and see you, was he?
Robert:	Did you love him?
Joan:	Don't be ridiculous.
Robert:	Stop acting!
Joan:	I loved how he made me feel, I told you. For those moments when he took the pain away. Are you happy now?
Robert:	Did Mum know? About you and him?
Joan:	Of course not. I never told her.
Robert:	(*to Tofi*) Did you?
Tofi:	I didn't have to.
	Joan looks at Tofi.
	She had eyes, Joan. She knew.
Joan:	She never said.

Robert: All this time—all this hate—because he chose Mum over you? That's low. Even for you.

Joan: Grow up, Robert. If you think I'm that pathetic then you really don't know me at all. Because that's not where the story ends.

Robert: Well? Where does it end, then? Tell me.

Joan: No. I shouldn't have said anything.

Robert: Uh-uh. You can't flop something like that out on the table and then not tell me. That's against the rules.

Joan: Take it from me, there are things you don't need to know.

Tofi: No, if there is something else, you should tell him.

Joan: You just keep your big nose out of this, alright, chief?

Tofi: 'Then you will know the truth and the truth will set you free.'

Joan: Enough with the God talk, you Pacific Island Buddha.

Joan pours a drink but Robert grabs it.

Robert: Come on, let's get it all out.

Joan: Give that back to me.

Robert: Not until you tell me.

Joan: Why did you have to invite him here today, Robert?

Robert: JUST. TELL. ME!

Joan takes a beat, steadies herself . . .

Joan: I came home . . . The day after he left. The day after he found out she was pregnant with you. I came home. There she was. In the bath. Red everywhere. I can't stand the sight of blood to this day. I didn't even know she was pregnant until the doctors told me. For a while there, it looked like we might lose both of you, but . . .

Robert: No.

Joan: Now do you understand, Robert? Why I find this so difficult? Why I've always found it so difficult. That you would have anything to do with this man. You and your mother almost died because of this man.

Robert: No. You're acting.

Joan: I'm not. You know I'm not.

Robert: She would have told me.

Joan: She never wanted you to know, Robert. Neither did I.

Robert: Oh, Mum . . .

Tofi: Why didn't anybody tell me this? You should have told me.

Joan: You weren't there to tell. You weren't there to scrub the blood from the bath. You weren't there to bandage her wrists. You weren't there to wipe away her tears. You weren't there to tell her everything was going to be alright. You weren't there to see her scars slowly fade away, but never completely. You weren't there to see her smile at her boy with sadness in her eyes. But I was. I was there. I was there to hate you so that she didn't have to. Why didn't anybody tell you, Tofi? Because you weren't there.

Tofi: I'm so sorry, Joan. I'm so sorry.

Tofi cries.

Robert: I think I'm going to be sick.

Joan: Just breathe, kid. Breathe.

A beat. Joan begins to pour herself a drink.

'Make me a willow cabin at your gate.

And call upon my soul within the house—'

She tops up Robert's drink.

'—Write loyal cantons of contemned love

And sing them loud even in the dead of night—'

She's about to sit down but then she tops up Tofi's drink.

'Halloo . . .'

She pauses, overcome with emotion.

'Halloo your name to the reverberate hills

And make the babbling gossip of the air

Cry out "Olivia".'

Joan raises her glass.

Tofi and Robert stand.

Tofi/Robert: Olivia.

The trio clink glasses.

They drink.

They stand for a moment, then Joan looks over at Gary.

Joan: (*nods*) Gary.

Darkness.

The End

Club Paradiso

Almost twenty years ago I saw a young Samoan actor running round in a lavalava in a production of David Williamson's *Heretic*. Even though he didn't have to do much more than look good in said lavalava I could sense he had a lot more to offer. I asked him to be in a reading of my play *Sons*; subsequently we played the titular brothers in a production for which he won best newcomer at the Chapman Tripp Theatre Awards in 1998.

So began my professional relationship with Robbie Magasiva. It's been the most significant professional relationship I've had in the theatre. Robbie's been both a muse and an alter ego: since *Sons* I have written four plays for him and he's managed to bring his enormous and often under-utilised range to each of them; be it playing a gay actor mistaken for a rapist in *Ranterstantrum*, a young man bent on destroying his birth father's family in *My Name is Gary Cooper* or an absent father who has to face some home truths in *At the Wake*.

The idea for *Club Paradiso* came after I asked Robbie what kind of role he'd like to play but hadn't yet had the chance to. He thought about it for a moment and then said he hadn't played someone evil.

Soon afterwards I went to stay with a friend in Los Angeles and wrote Club Paradiso in their spare room over a couple of days.

Dabbling with the darkness was a challenge: writing *Club Paradiso* is the only time as a writer that I've had to ask myself 'Can I bring myself to type the thought I just had in my head?' I'm glad the answer was 'yes': *Club Paradiso* may just be the play I'm most proud of.

When I gave Robbie the script, I warned him: Careful what you wish for.

Ultimately the performance Robbie gave as Q, the sadistic psychopath at the heart of *Club Paradiso*, was truly was one for the ages. Chilling, unpredictable, hard to watch and yet at the same time impossible to turn away from.

It's been a pleasure watching that young man in a lavalava who ran around in the background of *Heretic* almost twenty years ago transform into one of the most interesting lead actors working today. Malo, Lopaki.

—Victor Rodger

This play proves that Victor Rodger sits amongst our very top playwrights in Aotearoa New Zealand. *Club Paradiso* was, for me, a profound theatre experience, as it was for those others who were fortunate enough to see it during its short but potent season.

It is a play with strong dramatic action which keeps you guessing until its final climax. It was a well staged production. The direction was excellent and the actors responded to the demands of the script. You could feel their commitment to the playwright's ideas and concepts.

The audience was stunned by the concepts of the play. The play finished. (Silence.) The actors left the stage. (Silence.) The actors returned for a curtain call. (Still silence.) The actors bowed and then the audience erupted—it was no surprise to me, just a great pleasure that the audience could sense the quality of what was being offered by Victor and the production.

Victor Rodger is fearless. His writing encompasses you. He challenges an audience and the audience embraces his concepts. You are left with much food for thought. It is a profoundly interesting play.

—Raymond Hawthorne, ONZM

For Michael Tuitasi and Tatiana Gros-Desirs

Club Paradiso premiered in 2015 at the Basement Theatre in Auckland. It was produced by Leki Jackson-Bourke and Gaby Solomona for FCC with the following cast and production team:

Q	Robbie Magasiva
Tahlz	Anapela Polataivao
Bubbles	Amanaki Prescott-Faletau
Si	Levon Rawiri
Ave	Hans Masoe
Dante	Gabriel Halatoa
Sasha	Sandy Vukalokalo
Voice of Leighton	Emilio Tuala

Director	Vela Manusaute
Wardrobe Supervisor	Lucia Farron
Lighting Designer:	Suivai Autagavaia

Club Paradiso

Darkness.

Part of John Charles's score for The Quiet Earth *plays (from 1:07–1:32).*

Five characters enter:

Sasha (20s, a queen bee fafa) and Bubbles (20s, her right-hand fafa) take a seat at a table full of empty glasses.

Dante (18, a shy boy) hangs back uncertainly.

Ave (20s, very masculine) stands looking at the entrance of the club . . .

. . . and Tahlz (40s, voluptuous and sexy, but still very Earth-mother) stands behind the bar.

The set's simple: a table; some chairs; a karaoke machine; and a hand-drawn poster proclaiming CLUB PARADISO, with the O in the shape of a coconut.

As the music reaches a climax, the characters all look towards the entrance of the bar as if something—or someone—ominous is approaching.

The music ends abruptly.

Instantly the lights come on.

Sasha and Bubbles wince at the bright lights.

Sasha: Jesus Christ Superstar.

Bubbles:	Turn out the light. Turn out the light.
Ave:	(*shouting at offstage customers*) . . . and if I see your black mulis in here again, that's it.
Bubbles:	Girl, can you see any stubble?
Sandy:	Please Jesus, let me have my sunnies.

Sasha begins to fish around in her handbag.

Tahlz:	(*to Ave*) Son . . .
Ave:	You don't come here and disrespect my bar like that . . . (*under his breath*) fucking ufas.
Tahlz:	Ave, stop it. That's enough.
Ave:	Little shits, smoking P in the bogs.
Sasha:	I would too, to cope with that stink.
Ave:	What'd you say?
Tahlz:	They're gone. Okay? Let's just clean up and get out of here. It's been a long night.
Ave:	You were tired before we got here.
Tahlz:	(*under her breath*) Yeah, well if you were a solo mum running this place . . .
Ave:	What?
Tahlz:	Nothing.
Ave:	No, what?
Tahlz:	Let's just get this done, okay? Se vave.

Sasha finds her sunnies.

Sasha:	Thank you, Jesus! Thank you, Lord!

She puts them on.

Bubbles:	Yaaaaaas, queen. Hallelujah, girl.
Sasha/Bubbles:	Amene, girl.

Dante joins Tahlz.

Dante: Mum, what shall I do?

Ave: What the fuck do you think? Clean shit up.

Tahlz: Ave! It's his first shift. Leave him alone.

Ave: Ah, c'mon, Dante's not a baby. He can figure it out.

Tahlz: Just grab all the empties then empty the bottle bins, okay my baby?

Dante: 'Kay.

Ave watches Dante move off.

Ave: I'm sure he's a fafa.

Tahlz: You are such a vale sometimes.

Who cares? Dante's my son. Your brother. He can do whatever the hell he likes as long as he doesn't hurt anyone else.

Ave: Just saying.

Tahlz: Uckkkkk. Hurry up.

Tahlz moves off.

Sasha: Hey, so where were we?

Bubbles: Uh . . . okay, so you said you'd fuck Sonny Bill Williams . . . ?

Sasha: I'd so fuck Sonny Bill Williams . . .

Bubbles: Get down on it, girl.

Sasha: I'd marry Ma'a Nonu so we could share mascara. And I'd kill Dan Carter.

Bubbles: But he's so cute.

Sasha: Girl, you know I don't do white.

Bubbles: Leighton is white.

Sasha: Your husband?

Bubbles pulls up a photo of Leighton on her phone.

Bubbles: (*to photo*) I love you, honey.

She kisses the photo.

Sasha: Lemme see?

Sasha checks it out.

Not bad. For a palagi.

Bubbles: He'll be here soon.

Sasha: He's driving all the way to Flat Bush from Albany to pick your ass up? Must be love.

Bubbles: Maybe it is, girl.

Sasha: Like, for real?

Bubbles: He's a nice guy. A really nice guy.

Sasha: Oh-em-gee. You're actually in love. Uccck. I so hate your guts right now.

Bubbles: Don't hate: celebrate, sister-girl.

Sasha: Ia, celebrate this.

Sasha gives Bubbles the finger.

The girls laugh.

Ave: C'mon, youse need to finish your drinks, please.

Sasha raises her Vodka Cruiser to Ave and deliberately gives him a sweet smile.

Sasha: Ia, manuia.

But when he's out of earshot . . .

E, aikae.

Bubbles: One more Fuck, Marry, Kill?

Sasha: Hit it.

Bubbles: Mike Hosking . . .

Sasha:	Gross.
Bubbles:	John Key.
Sasha:	I'm going to be sick.
Bubbles:	Gerry Brownlee.

Sasha pretends to vomit all over herself.

So?

Sasha:	Hello? Suicide. As if I'd let any of those polos touch these. Oh my gosh, yuck to infinity squared.

Sasha catches Dante listening in.

Bubbles:	Who'd you fuck, marry and kill, sole?
Dante:	What?
Ave:	Let's go, Dante.

Sasha looks around the bar.

Sasha:	You know what, sis? We should be in Paris or New York, drinking Cristal, wearing Dior, darling, saying 'No photos, no photos . . .'
Bubbles:	Yassssssss, queen!
Sasha:	Instead of having ready-mades in this dump. Flat Bush. Who the hell called it Flat Bush in the first place? They may as well have called it Squashed Pussy.
Dante:	Are youse done?
Sasha:	Hey, this vodka cost eight bucks. It's not going anywhere until it's all inside me. Lucky vodka!

Dante moves off to clear some other glasses away.

Hey, sole. You wanna hear a joke?

Dante:	Sure.
Sasha:	A man walks into a bar. And he's like, 'I'm celebrating my first blowjob! Gimme five shots of tequila!' And

the barman, he's like, 'Congratulations! Have one on me.' But then the guy says, 'If five shots of tequila don't get rid of the taste, I doubt six will work either.'

Dante: What? I don't get it.

Sasha: Are you sure?

Sasha and Bubbles dissolve into laughter . . . but Dante, uncomfortable, moves off.

Poor little GG.

Tahlz overhears.

Tahlz: What's a GG?

Dante looks at Sasha nervously.

Sasha: Nothing. It's just a—y'know—a Good Guy.

Tahlz: You are a GG, aren't you, my darling?

Dante: Mum, don't.

Tahlz: What? Can't I call my own son a GG?

Ave: Okay time to finish your drinks, guys.

Sasha: 'Guys'? Hel-lo? We're ladies. Lady Sasha.

Bubbles: Lady Bubbles.

Ave: Whatever you are, it's time to go home. Or hit the corner. Whatever.

Bubbles: I'm waiting for my husband to pick me up, thank you very much.

Sasha: Same. Maybe you've heard of him? His name's Sonny? Sonny Bill Williams?

The girls laugh.

Ave: In your dreams, bro.

Sasha: (*imitating Ave*) 'Bro'? (*in a super masculine voice, to Bubbles*) Okay, bro. Let's scull this piss and gap it, eh?

Then let's go find us some pussy.

The girls dissolve into giggles. Tahlz laughs too.

(*in a masculine voice*) Hey, bro, you gonna come look for some puss-puss with us, bro?

Ave: Fuck's sake.

Tahlz: Hey.

Ave: What?

Tahlz: Calm your farm, alright? They're just having a bit of fun.

Ave: You're the one who's been saying all night that you're tired and you want to get home. The sooner we get them outta here, the sooner we can go home.

Tahlz: Life is about choices, Ave. You can choose to be polite. Or you can choose to be a polo. Just saying.

Sasha: (*sotto*) Yassssssss, queen. Preach.

Bubbles: Take it to *church*, Mama.

Dante giggles. Ave rounds on him.

Ave: You think that's funny?

Tahlz: Leave Dante alone. And you leave them alone too. Ladies, you take your time.

Bubbles: Tai lava, Tahlz.

Sasha: Oooooh, does that mean we can do one more song on the karaoke?

Ave: No.

Tahlz: Go for it.

Ave looks exasperated.

Choices, Ave. Choices.

Ave: Yeah, well I'm choosing to be pissed off right now.

Tahlz: And I'm choosing to finish cleaning up this bar so we
            can all go home.

            *Sasha saunters over to the karaoke machine, grabs the
            microphone dramatically and does some sexual heavy-
            breathing into the mic.*

Sasha: Testing, testing.

            Good evening, Flat Bush! Can you hear me?

Bubbles: Yassssss, girl, we can *hear* you!

Sasha: You've been a fan*tas*tic audience. We've got time for
            one more song . . . when I can find it.

            Sasha looks through the karaoke playlist.

            Ave looks over at the bar doors.

Ave: Did you hear that?

Tahlz: Hear what?

            Tahlz sees that Ave is tense.

            Hey. C'mere.

            She runs a finger down the middle of his frown.

            We'll be home soon.

            A warm moment until . . .

Sasha: (*in a masculine voice*) Hey, bro. Bro, this one's for
            you, bro.

            Sasha punches in a number on the karaoke machine.

            'How Will I Know' by Whitney Houston begins to play.

            Tahlz tries to stifle a laugh.

Ave: Fucking hell.

Tahlz: Choose happy, Ave. Choose happy.

            *Sasha begins to sing along and incorporates some
            comical, over-the-top movement.*

At one point she holds the mic out to Bubbles.

Bubbles sings the appropriate line of the song.

Sasha sings some more then holds the mic out to Ave.

Ave: Fuck, as if.

Sasha then holds the mic out to Tahlz, who happily sings the appropiate line of the song.

Tahlz: (*to Ave, over Sasha singing*) See? Your mum's still got it.

Sasha continues to sing then holds the mic out to Dante.

Dante: I don't know it, sorry.

Sasha: Awesome!

She's about to continue the song, when suddenly: a big bang (offstage).

Dante drops a couple of empty Vailima bottles.

What the hell was that?

Ave: If it's those fucking P-heads . . .

Ave disappears out the bar doors.

Tahlz: It was probably just an exhaust pipe?

The music continues to play.

Ave?

Silence.

Ave?

Everyone looks towards the bar doors.

Ave reappears, his back to everyone.

What was it?

Ave walks in backwards.

Q follows him in (40s, tattooed, mean-looking).

Q's in a ripped white T-shirt; a T-shirt covered in blood.

He's holding a gun, aimed at Ave.

Q: Turn that shit off.

Dante turns the karaoke off.

Bubbles's phone begins to ring. The ringtone is something by Beyoncé.

Q swings the gun at Bubbles.

Sasha drops her microphone.

Q swings the gun at Sasha.

As the phone continues to ring, Sasha tries to appear unfazed.

Q's face breaks out into a dangerous smile.

Not scared of the big bad wolf?

Sasha: Should I be?

Q: You got balls.

Q laughs.

Get it?

Tahlz: You want money? Whatever you need . . .

Q: Fuck money.

Ave: What do you want, uso?

Q: I'm not your fucking uso, cunt.

Ave: Okay.

Q: We related?

Ave: No, we're—

Q: We know each other?

Ave: I'm sorry, I was just—

Q: So I'm not your fucking uso.

Ave: Okay. Okay. My bad.

Q runs a hand over his face, then looks down at his hand—it's covered in blood.

He notices that Bubbles is freaked.

Q: You don't like blood? Don't worry. It's not mine.

Q licks some blood off his fingers.

Wanna taste?

He moves towards Bubbles. Goes to put his bloody finger in her mouth.

Bubbles knees him in the nuts.

Everyone follows Bubbles offstage as she bolts for the back door.

Run all you like, you stupid fafa.

Suddenly we hear screams.

Everyone reappears with another man, Si (mixed race, a bit slow), who has his gun pointed to Bubbles's head.

Si: Should I shoot her, Q? Should I? Is it my turn, now? Huh? Is it? Is it my turn?

Fahhhhhh. Man, when you shot that cop, that was mean, uso. Mean. 'Don't shoot me, I got a wife and two kids.' Boom. BOOM!

So is it my turn?

Q: Nah, let her go.

Si: Fahhhhh . . . .

Q walks over to Bubbles.

Q: Welcome back. Afio mai.

He smiles.

Sasha: Don't hurt her.

Q turns to Sasha.

Q: Or what?

Q joins Sasha.

What's your name?

Sasha: Sasha.

Q: That's not your name. What's your real name?

Sasha: I told you, it's Sasha.

Q sighs.

Q: I'm just trying to get know my new buddies. So let's try that again. Malo lava, suga. I'm Q. What's your name?

Sasha: It's Sasha.

Q laughs, then suddenly points his gun at Sasha's head.

Q: Last chance.

Bubbles: Just tell him, Sasha.

Ave: For Christ's sake . . .

Tahlz: Just do what he says.

A moment where it looks like Sasha will relent . . .

Sasha: My name is . . . My name is . . .

Q: Come on, bro.

Sasha: My name is Fuck. You.

Silence.

Q begins to laugh.

And laugh.

And laugh.

Until he points the gun at Sasha's face and shoots her point blank.

Bubbles: Sasha! No-no-no-no-no-no-no-no-no . . .

Sasha falls to the ground, makes some gasping sounds.
Bubbles kneels by her side.

Si: My turn now? My turn, sole Q? My turn?

Q: Fa'akali.

Tahlz: Suga, it's okay. It's okay. We're here.

Bubbles: Hold on, Sasha. We'll get you some help, it's going to be okay.

Q: That's a Tui ad right there . . .

Bubbles: Sasha? Sasha? Sasha?

Bubbles holds Sasha's hand tight . . .

. . . until Sasha becomes still and her hand falls to the floor.

Bubbles stares at the body.

Si: She's dead, eh?

Tahlz: Yes. She's dead.

Si gets excited.

Si: That's two! Two! Auoia! You go 'bang' and then the fafa goes (*he imitates Sasha getting shot*). Just like the cop.

Tahlz, Dante, Ave and Bubbles look at each other.

You shoulda seen it, the cop was like, 'Drop your weapon.' (*laughs*) 'Drop your weapon,' and you just go *bang* and he goes, like, 'I got a wife and two kids,' and then you go . . .

Q: *Bang*!

Si: . . . and he . . .

Si imitates the cop getting shot.

And that look on his face. Like this—

Si does an expression of surprise.

You the man, Q, you the man . . .

Q surveys the others menacingly.

Q: Yeah. That's right. I'm the man. The man going out
          with a bang.

Si: With a bang, eh, Q.

Q: *Big Bang Theory.* Youse watch that show? Stupid
          palagis. But that chick, that palagi chick. I'd fuck her.

Si: Going out with a bang.

Q: Yeah, we're going out with a bang 'cause that's the
          only way to go out, right, uso?

Si: You the man, Q. You the man.

          Q looks from Tahlz to Dante to Ave to Bubbles . . .

Q: Right. Eeeney, meeney, miney . . .

          . . . until he settles on Dante.

          You.

Tahlz: No, please, that's my son.

Q: Your son? You sure he's not your daughter?

Tahlz: Please don't hurt him.

          Q points the gun in Dante's direction.

Q: What's your name?

Dante: Dante.

Q: What the fuck kind of name is that?

          Silence.

          You fucken mute? I asked you a question.

Dante: I don't know. It's just my name.

Q: Dante? What does that make you think of, Si?

Si:	Dante? Dan. Te. Darn. Darn it. Sewing. I don't know. That's a hard one, Q.
Q:	Clean up that mess, Dante.

Dante tentatively walks over to the bar and grabs some cloths and cleaning spray.

	What the fuck are you doing?
Dante:	You said clean up the mess.
Q:	You fucking with me, sole?
Dante:	No.
Q:	You taking the piss?
Dante:	No.

Q presses the gun right against Dante's head.

Q:	I'm not here to play. You got that?
Dante:	Sorry. I'm sorry. I don't know what you mean.
Tahlz:	Don't hurt him. Please, don't hurt him.
Q:	YOU GOT THAT?
Dante:	Yes.
Q:	Let's try that again, you little faggot. Clean up that mess.

Dante is still unsure what Q means.

C'mon, figure it out, fucker. Figure it out . . .

Uncertain, Dante grabs Sasha's legs and prepares to drag her out.

Good girl. And don't even think of running out the back or I'm gonna blow Big Mama's brains out and then I'm gonna make you get rid of that mess too, you hear me?

Dante nods.

Now clean that shit up.

Everyone watches as Dante drags Sasha offstage.

Bubbles begins to cry.

Bubbles: Sasha . . .

Q: Awwww, what's wrong, bubba?

Bubbles: Sasha was my best friend.

Q: Oh yeah? Well she isn't anymore, is she? 'Cause she's dead.

Q laughs.

Better make a new friend, uh. You wanna be friends with me? You wanna be friends with Q?

Bubbles trembles.

Ave: What do you want, man?

Q: Was I talking to you?

Ave: No.

Q: So why the fuck are you talking to me? If I wanna hear from your ugly black cunt muli, I'll tell you.

Ave: Okay, okay.

Q: That attitude in your voice? Sounds like attitude. I don't like attitude. Makes you sound like a bitch. Are you a bitch?

Ave: No.

Q: You sound like a bitch. You sure you're not a bitch?

Ave: It's all good.

Q laughs.

Q: 'It's all good'? You hear that, Si? Listen to this ufa . . .

Dante returns. Blood on his hands. He looks down at it.

Sticky, eh, blood? You wanna go wash it off?

Dante: Is that okay?

Q: Sit the fuck down.

Dante joins Tahlz. She wipes the blood off his hands.

Mummy make it all better. Awwwwww.

Q takes out a P pipe and lights it.

Lights change. The Quiet Earth *music plays again.*

Q smokes, then gives the pipe to Si.

Si smokes.

Anyone else?

He offers the pipe.

Silence.

Whatever.

Lights change. Q looks around the bar.

You wanna know something, guys? Today's a special day here at Club Paradiso. You know why? 'Cause it's my birthday today.

Silence.

Well, aren't you gonna sing me happy birthday?

Silence.

FUCKING SING ME HAPPY BIRTHDAY, YOU CUNTS.

Bubbles/Tahlz/Dante/Ave: (*staggered and not in unison*) Happy birthday to you / Happy birthday to you / Happy birthday dear . . .

Silence.

Q: Q. Jesus Christ, Q. It's one letter. Fuck!

Bubbles/Tahlz/Dante/Ave: Q. Happy birthday to you.

Q: What do you think, Si?

Si: I don't know, Q.

Q: Do you think they really sounded like they want me
            to have a happy birthday?

Si: I don't think so, Q.

Q: I don't think so either, Si. So what do you think I
            should do about that? Do you think I should punish
            them?

Si: Teach them a lesson?

Q: Yeah. Teach them a lesson. I think that's a good idea,
            Si. Teach them to . . .

Ave: Teach me a lesson. Let them go and teach me a
            lesson . . . ?

            Silence.

Tahlz: Son—don't.

Q: Puffing out your chest. Dropping your voice. Trying
            to be the man. But you aren't the man. I'm the man. I
            been through shit you couldn't even imagine in your
            worst fucking nightmare. I had a dick my arse before
            I was three. I'd give you two seconds inside before
            you were screaming like a girl. I know your type.
            Think you're tough. But you don't know tough. You
            don't know dick.

            Ave glowers.

            What? You not going to say anything? You want to
            though, uh? You wanna tell me to go fuck myself.
            Well fuck you, you pussy motherfucker.

            *Ave clearly wants to have a go at Q but Tahlz silently
            implores him not to.*

            Yeah. Knew you were a pussy. And speaking of
            pussy . . .

            He approaches Tahlz, looks her up and down.

Ave: You touch my mum, I'll kill you.

                Q playfully touches Tahlz on the arm.

Q: Touched her.

                He touches her again.

                Touched her again.

                Q touches her again on the shoulder, then slowly lets his finger trace a line from her shoulder to her breast.

Tahlz: Ave, don't do anything. I'm alright.

                His finger continues to move down Tahlz's body . . .

Q: Look at that, Si. I'm still alive. It's a miracle.

                Q's about to touch her crotch when Bubbles's phone goes.

                Everyone looks at the phone.

                Q begins to dance and lip sync to the song as he makes his way over to the phone.

                The phone keeps ringing.

                Q picks it up and looks at the caller ID.

                (*reading*) Leighton? Who the fuck's that?

                Bubbles hesitates.

Bubbles: My boyfriend. He's here to pick me up.

                Q answers the phone.

Q: Hey. (*listens*) Bubbles? Yeah, she's here. You wanna speak to her? She's, uh, she's a bit busy, brother.

                Q hangs up.

                The phone starts ringing again.

                Someone knocks at the door.

                Q hangs up.

                Well, bring him in. Let's get this party started.

Leighton:	(*offstage*) Bubbles?

Q points his gun at Bubbles's head.

Q:	You say anything, they're all dead. You know I'm not playing.

Bubbles goes to the bar doors.

Leighton:	(*offstage*) Bubbles, I know you're in there? Hello?
Bubbles:	Go home, Leighton.
Leighton:	Who was that who answered your phone?
Bubbles:	Leighton . . .
Leighton:	Can you open up? Come on, let's go.
Bubbles:	I said go home, Leighton.
Leighton:	Hey, if this is a joke, it's not funny. I just drove all the way from Albany. I bought that Double Quarter Pounder like you asked. Mayo. Steamed bun. No pickle.
Bubbles:	Fuck off. Go. I mean it. We're done.

She touches the bar door, almost as if she could reach through the door and somehow touch Leighton.

Leighton:	Are you serious?
Bubbles:	Just go home, Leighton. I've met someone else.

Bubbles is trying not to cry.

Leighton:	What are you talking about . . . ?
Bubbles:	Just go the fuck home to Mummy and Daddy on the shore, motherfucker. I'm over it.
Leighton:	I don't get it. You were fine just before. Where did this all come—
Bubbles:	Are you *deaf*? I said, *over it*. Get out of here, already. *Go*!
Leighton:	Fuck you, Bubbles.

Silence.

Bubbles turns back to the others, crying.

Q: Poor baby crying. Stop it. Suck it in. Suck, suck, suck it in . . .

You fafas, you all suck a mean dick, I'll give you that. You love it, uh? Sucking dick?

Bubbles trembles.

That's what all you fafas dream about, isn't it? Some big dick in your mouth?

Did your boyfriend have a big dick? Your ex-boyfriend, I mean.

Tahlz: Leave her alone. Just tell us what you want from us?

Q: I told you. It's my birthday. I wanna celebrate. I wanna have fun. I want everyone to have fun. You having fun, guys?

Silence.

Q throws a chair across the room.

ARE YOU FUCKING HAVING FUN?

Tahlz: Yes. We're having fun.

Q: Fucking liar.

Ave glares at Q.

What? What? What? Yeah, that's right . . .

I know. How 'bout you guys sing me another song? But it's gotta be better than when you sang me 'Happy Birthday'. 'Cause that was—that was shit.

Si: What song, Q?

Q: Any song.

Silence.

Q raises his gun, points it at Tahlz.

Three, two—

Dante leaps to his feet begins to sing 'In Da Club' by 50 Cent.

Dante: 'Go, go, go, go go, go, go, shawty / It's your birthday.'

Q: Ha ha ha, shot, sole.

Dante: 'We gon' party like it's yo birthday / We gon' sip Bacardi like it's your birthday / And you know we don't give a fuck / It's not your birthday!

Q: Everybody up. Dancing.

Everybody gets up and moves to Dante's beat.

Dante: 'You can find me in the club, bottle full of bub / Look mami I got the X if you into taking drugs / I'm into having sex, I ain't into making love / So come give me a hug if you . . .'

Q: (*taking over*) '. . . if you into getting rubbed.'

Q looks directly at Tahlz.

Dante stops singing.

Rub-a-dub-dub.

Q grabs Tahlz's breasts while looking directly at Ave.

Tahlz: Father God . . .

Q: Ahhh, Jesus. Talk about spoiling it.

Tahlz: Why?

Q: Why what?

Tahlz: This bar. Why'd you choose this bar?

Q shrugs.

Q: The lights were on.

Tahlz: That's it?

Q: Yeah. Fuck, who cares? We're here now. And we're not going anywhere . . .

Q looks around the club.

Club Paradiso, huh?

What's it make you think of, Si? That name? Club Paradiso?

Si: Paradiso? Para. Diso. Para. Noia? Para. Chute? Para. Plegic?

Q: Club Paraplegic? That's a good one, Si.

Si: Yeah, you like that, Q?

Q: Yeah. Do you think we should turn this into Club Paraplegic, Si?

Si: What do you mean?

Q: Should we turn someone into a paraplegic?

Si: Yeah, Q, that sounds like fun.

Q: Who do you think that lucky person should be? Dwayne Johnson over here? Or Teuila Blakely over there? What about you, Medea? Or how about you, Junior?

Tahlz: Who are you?

Q: I'm the big bad fucken wolf, that's who.

Tahlz: We haven't done anything to you.

Q: Told you. We're going out with a bang. We busted loose this week, right Si?

Si: Over that wall.

Q: No way, we're going back. Right, Si?

Never going back. Been inside that shithole ten years. Fucked if I'm going back.

Si? Which one? You choose.

Si looks at the others.

Si: I don't know. That's hard.

Q spies an empty bottle of Vailima on the ground and walks over to it.

Q: I only remember one birthday party my whole life. Some aunty, I forget who.

Tahlz: Someone who cared about you?

Q: She had a birthday party for me. And there was this one game I remember . . .

Tahlz: You don't have to do this.

Q: Everyone in a circle.

Nobody moves.

I said everyone get in a fucking circle.

Bubbles, Dante, Tahlz and Ave form a circle.

Spread out. I SAID SPREAD OUT.

Q walks into the middle of the circle.

Now let's see who's gonna be the new face of Club Paraplegic.

Q puts the bottle in the middle of the circle.

He spins it.

Silence.

There's just the sound of the bottle spinning round and round and round . . . until it points to whichever character it points to.

Q talks to whoever it is.

C'mere.

The character doesn't move.

Q points the gun at them.

I said, C'mere!

The character joins Q.

How shall I do it, Si?

Si: I don't know, Q.

Q: Jump on their back? Yeah. Jump on their back. Like I did to that kefe, Vili.

Si: Yeah, Q. And he never got up again, eh? Lie down. Right, on the count of three. One . . .

Q winks at Si.

Si jumps.

Two.

Si jumps again.

Three.

Si doesn't jump.

The character looks petrified.

Q looks at them for a beat, then laughs.

Q: Hey, hey, hey. Look at me. You really think I'd turn someone into a paraplegic? What kind of monster do you think I am? You think I'm a monster? I'm not a monster. The screws were monsters. My mum was a monster. My dad was a monster. The cop was a monster. Fucking pig. One less pig in the world now, right, Si?

Si: Yeah, Q. One less pig.

Si squeals like a pig.

Q: Here piggy wiggy, here piggy wiggy.

Si squeals like a pig then pretends to get shot and fall down dead.

Q trains the gun on everyone, settling on Dante.

You—introduce me to your mates?

Dante: That's my mum, Tahlz. That's my big brother, Ave. I don't really know her.

Q: What's your name?

Bubbles: Bubbles.

Q: That's not your name. I know that's not your name. So lemme ask you again, what's your name? And don't even think about giving me the same answer that your friend did, 'cause we all know how that turned out.

Bubbles: Nuku.

Q: Tongan? Well, fēfē hake?

Bubbles: Sai pē.

Q: Ahhh, mālō 'aupito. (Mata'usi.)

Si/Q: (*singing*) So mata'usi right now / So mata'usi right now / So mata'usi right now . . .

They stomp their feet on the beat, getting louder and louder until Q suddenly stops.

Q: Time for another birthday game.

Si: What's the game, Q?

Q: Musical chairs. But just a quick game. One round.

Si: Can I play?

Q: Sure. Why not? Why don't you help me? Five of you, so four chairs in a circle.

Si helps Q organise the chairs.

Si: How do we play?

Q walks over to some turntables.

Q: I play some music. And everyone moves around the chairs. And when the music stops, everyone has to sit on a chair. But if you don't sit on a chair, then . . .

Si: Then what happens?

Q: That's a surprise, uso.

Si: I like surprises.

Ave: Listen, is this really—?

Q: Shut your fucking mouth you pots cunt or I'm gonna find a needle and a thread and I'm gonna get your mum to sew your ju-ju lips together.

Si: Yay, game time. I love games.

Q: Yeah, they're fun, uh, sole?

Okay. Everybody ready?

Tahlz, Ave, Dante and Bubbles look at each other uncertainly, but Si is excited.

Here we go.

Bill Sevesi's 'Time Out Steel Guitar' begins to play. Q pretends like he's at a rodeo and grabs the karaoke microphone.

Round and round and round they go. Yee-har!

Si joins in the game wholeheartedly, circling the chairs.

The others shuffle around, uncertain.

What the fuck? This isn't an old people's home. Fucking move.

Everyone picks up the pace.

Faster.

They move faster.

Faster!

They move even faster.

I said faaaaaassssssterrrrrr!

Everyone moves really fast until Bubbles trips over.

Dante helps her to her feet.

They keep running around the chairs . . .

Suddenly the music stops.

Si darts to an empty chair.

Si: Yay! I got a chair.

. . . but no one else moves.

Q: This is my fucking birthday. Play by the fucking
             rules.

He raises his gun, points it at the others.

Ave: (*to Tahlz*) Go.

Tahlz looks over at Dante.

Tahlz: Dante . . .

Q: What the fuck is this?

Tahlz: Dante do it, just sit.

Dante takes a seat.

(*to Bubbles*) You too.

Bubbles takes a seat.

*Tahlz and Ave take each other's hand, look into each
other's eyes.*

Now you.

Ave: No way.

Tahlz: I mean it, son. You do what I tell you.

Ave: Okay, Mum. Okay.

*It looks like Ave has relented. But instead, Ave grabs
Tahlz and marches her over to the last remaining seat.*

Tahlz: Stop it, Ave, let me go. Ave! I said let me go!

Ave forces Tahlz to sit. Ave stands back, faces Q.

Q claps.

Q: Finally. Some polos. Good for you, fucker. Good for you.

Ave: I love you, Mum.

Tahlz: I love you too, son.

Ave grabs Dante.

Ave: If anything happens, it's on you, Dante. You got that? You got it?

Dante: Yes.

Tahlz: Q? Please. Don't do this.

Q: But you don't know what I'm about to do. It might be something nice. It might be something you enjoy.

Tahlz: It's okay, son, everything's going to be okay.

Q laughs. And laughs. And laughs.

Then suddenly stops.

He moves over towards Tahlz.

Puts his hand on her stomach.

Q: Why the fuck you want to bring kids into this shit world? Huh?

Tahlz: I love my kids. With all my heart. Always have, from the moment they came into this world. These boys— nothing but love for them. Always.

Q: The only thing my mother loved was whoever bought her next fucking drink or her next fucking hit.

Tahlz: You've had a lot of pain in your life, I can see that. And I'm sorry you didn't have a mother who loved you.

Q: Fuck you, Dr Phil. Save your pity. You trying to *relate* to me? Get on my level?

| Tahlz: | You don't have to do this. This is a choice. You can choose not to do this. It's a choice. Don't you see? All of it. Everything's a choice. And there are reasons for those choices, I get that, but— |

Q roughly pulls back Tahlz's hair.

| Q: | Who the fuck do you think you are, eh? Who the fuck do you think you're talking to? You trying to *connect* with me? Trying to *get* me? You can't get me. Your mum put cigarettes out on your arm? Your dad break your leg then when you come home from the hospital, break your other? |

| Tahlz: | No. |

| Q: | All those CYFs fuckers? Sending me back there. I knew what was gonna happen. They knew what was gonna happen. I was fucken four years old. But I'm glad all of that happened to me. You know why? 'Cause it taught me something. You know what that is? Not to give a shit. About anyone. Anything. Nothing. No one. |

| Tahlz: | I'm sorry that happened to you, Q. I really am. |

| Q: | Bitch, you don't know me. You will never know me. |

| Si: | Yeah, you tell her, Q, you tell her. |

| Q: | So you quit trying to *get* me. You don't get to *get* me. Got it? |

Q pulls her hair back harder.

| Ave: | You get your hands off her. |

| Q: | Or what? C'mon, big man, or what? |

| Tahlz: | It's okay, Ave. I'm alright. |

But Q pulls her hair tighter, makes Tahlz scream.

| Q: | (*to Ave*) C'mon Muhammad Ali? Where have those polos gone now? Or they shrivelled up like a couple |

of peas? Aren't you gonna be a hero? Show Mummy here what you're made of?

Tahlz: Don't listen to him, Ave.

Ave: You've got a gun. Why don't you put it down and we can settle this. Old school. 'Cause this isn't fair. Not when you've got a gun. When he's (*Si*) got a gun.

Q: Fair? Who the fuck said anything about fair? Life isn't fair. Fair doesn't exist.

          Q pulls even harder on Tahlz's hair.

Ave: You're hurting her.

Q: So what are you going to do about it?

Tahlz: Don't, Ave.

          Ave looks coiled, ready to spring.

          Son, don't.

          Ave relents.

Q: Look at you. Mummy's boy. Yes, Mummy. No, Mummy. Three bags full, Mummy. Whipped, motherfucker. Ka-pish. Ka-fucken-pish.

          Ave suddenly rushes Q, tackles him to the ground.

Si: Hey! Q? What do I do?

          Ave struggles to dominate Q but Q slowly and surely gets the better of Ave and eventually flips him onto his stomach and pins him down.

Q: Yeah, nigga, you struggle all you like. You're not going anywhere. And we got all the time in the world, you and me. Eh, handsome? Eh?

          Q kisses Ave roughly on the ear.

          You like that? Yeah, I bet you like that. They'd like him inside, wouldn't they, Si? Pretty boy like this.

Ave continues to struggle.

I know what you're thinking. You're thinking, What's he gonna do to me? Is he gonna do what I think he's gonna do? Is he gonna do that in front of my mum? Wouldn't be like it was your first time though, right? Right?

Q tightens his grip around Ave's neck.

I mean a man like you, he must'a sucked dick before, right? Si. Gimme my gun.

Si gives Q his gun.

Q stands up and points the gun to Ave's temple.

Get up.

Ave gets up.

Q points the gun at Bubbles.

You, come here.

Bubbles joins Ave.

(*to Ave*) On your knees.

Ave stands still.

Tahlz: Do what he says, Ave.

Ave: Fuck that. He's gonna kill us anyway.

Tahlz: Don't give up. There's always hope. Always.

Ave: I'm not going out like this.

Q points his gun at Ave. Ave stays still.

Tahlz: Just do what he says!

Reluctantly, Ave gets down on his knees.

Q: Good boy, doing what Mummy says. Reward for good boy.

Q roughly grabs Bubbles.

You. C'mere.

Q rips off her panties and pulls up her skirt.

Now suck on that fucker.

Ave: Fuck you.

Q: What was that?

Ave: You heard me.

Q: No, sole. Fuck you.

Q marches over to Tahlz, puts the gun to her head and pulls the trigger back.

Five.

Tahlz: Ave!

Q: Four.

Tahlz: Father God, please.

Q: Three.

Si: Uh-oh.

Q: Two.

Ave: Mum . . .

Tahlz: Ave, do what he says!

Ave puts Bubbles's dick in his mouth.

Q laughs.

Q: Yeah. There you go. Now you suck that dick, you little cocksucker. You suck it. Now moan. Moan like the bitch you are.

Ave begins to moan.

You love it. Don't you? (*to Tahlz*) See? He loves it.

Ave stops sucking.

You stop when I tell you to stop, sole.

Ave resumes sucking Bubbles's dick.

Bubbles is crying.

Oh, is baby crying? What's the matter? I found you a new boyfriend. I'm a millionaire motherfucking matchmaker. You should be happy. You should be grateful.

Q puts the gun to Ave's head.

Moan, you bitch. Moan.

Ave moans with faux pleasure.

Louder!

Ave moans louder.

LOUDER!

But suddenly Ave is crying.

Awwww, now this baby is crying too. Gee, we got a lot of cry babies in Club Paraplegic. Little baby needs to suck on the dummy. That make little baby feel better.

Q flicks Bubbles on the head. Bubbles moans in terror.

You sucking on a dick. Why the fuck you crying? That's nothing, you little bitch. Nothing. You try being a kid, doing shit to strangers, having strangers do that shit to you. Suck it. Suck it. Suck it. Suck.

Tahlz: Why are you doing this?

Q: Because I can. Because I'm Q.

Si: The man.

Q: The motherfucking man. I'm where it starts and where it stops. The way, the truth and the light. I'm God. Almighty God. Down on your knees. EVERYONE.

Bubbles and Dante get down on their knees. Tahlz joins

Ave, who is still crying.

Tahlz: It's okay, son. It's okay.

Q: Close your eyes. Everybody close your eyes.

Dante: Mum? Is this it?

Tahlz: No, son. I won't let it be.

Q: CLOSE THEM!

Everyone closes their eyes.

And you lift your hands up to the Lord, your God. You lift your hands up to me. And you listen. Listen to the gospel . . . the word . . . listen . . .

The lights change.

'Hit 'Em Up' by 2Pac begins to play. It's like only Q can hear it.

Q dances with evil in his eyes, lost in the moment, arms spread like Christ.

Now get up and dance. Keep your eyes shut! Dance! Fucking dance!

Tahlz, Dante and Bubbles get up and dance.

Ave stays down.

The lights change.

Get up, freak.

Ave opens his eyes, glares at Q.

What? What? What? You want another go, mummy's boy? Don't be a silly billy.

Ave roars and lunges at Q.

Everyone opens their eyes.

Ave: Fuck you, you sick fuck!

Ave tackles Q to the ground.

Tahlz: Ave!

                  Tahlz goes to help Ave but Si points his gun at her.

Si: Back off.

                  Ave is giving it everything he's got, trying to overpower Q, trying desperately to wrestle control of the gun in Q's hand.

                  For a moment it looks like Ave has control of the gun and begins to point it in Q's face . . .

Ave: Fuck you, you sick cunt.

Q: I'm God, motherfucker. You hear me? I'm God. You can't beat God. Won't beat God. You can try all you like—it's not gonna happen.

                  . . . but slowly Q takes control of the gun and points it in Ave's direction.

Ave: Help me, Jesus.

Tahlz: Please, Jesus.

Q: Jesus isn't gonna help you, motherfucker. Jesus isn't here. Not in Club Paradiso. Not anywhere. He never helped me. And he's not going to help you!

                  Finally Q turns the gun around so it's right in Ave's face.

Tahlz: Ave!

Ave: Mum! Mum! I love—

                  Bang.

                  Q shoots Ave.

                  Ave falls back. Dead.

                  Tahlz screams in disbelief, rushes to kneel beside Ave's body.

                  Dante joins her.

Tahlz: Ave . . . Ave . . . oh, Ave . . . .

A moment where Tahlz tries to wipe blood from Ave's face.

Si looks on. This death seems to make him a little sad.

Si: Three. You the man, Q. You the man.

Beat.

Tahlz: I'm sorry.

Q is taken aback.

Q: You're sorry?

Tahlz continues to stroke Ave's face.

Tahlz: I'm sorry you've never really known love, have you? No one's ever really loved you, have they? But my Ave, he was loved. So loved.

She kisses Ave tenderly on the head.

Q: (*sarcastic*) Awwwww. Isn't that sweet, Si? Mummy loved Sonny. But Sonny's dead. Poor Mummy. We make Mummy feel better?

Bubbles sees Si is a little distracted and suddenly grabs Si's gun, then presses it against his temple.

Bubbles: Drop your gun. I mean it, motherfucker.

Q: What're you gonna do with that gun?

Bubbles: I'll use it. I swear to God.

Q: Didn't you listen to me? God isn't here, dumb-dumb.

Bubbles: You think I'm joking? I mean it. Now put your gun down.

But Q keeps moving towards Bubbles.

Drop it.

Q: You sound like someone off a cop show. I hate cop shows. The good guys always win. Stupid.

Q moves closer.

Bubbles: Don't come any closer. I mean it.

Q: You hear that, Si? The fafa means it. Guess we should be scared. Real scared.

Q is almost on top of Bubbles.

Bubbles: You take one more step, I'll blow his fucking brains out.

Q: You? Nah. You haven't got the balls. Not for that, anyway.

Bubbles: Fuck you.

Bubbles pulls the trigger . . . .

. . . but is horrified when the gun squirts water.

Bubbles's stomach falls. She's holding a water gun.

Oh my God.

Q gives Si his gun then takes Bubbles's water gun from her.

Q: Keep an eye on them.

Si: Where you going, Q?

Q: Gonna go have some fun. Gonna rip open my birthday present. Rip, rip, rip.

Bubbles lunges at Q, trying to scratch his face, but Q is too strong for her and just laughs.

Is that it? Is that all you got?

Bubbles continues to struggle.

Well, suga. Lemme show you what I got.

Q roughly hauls Bubbles offstage.

Bubbles: No, please . . .

Bubbles struggles with everything she has . . . but it's not enough.

A beat where Si is watching over Dante and Tahlz, who is still cradling Ave in her arms.

Dante: I'm sorry, Mum.

Tahlz: It's gonna be alright, son.

Suddenly Bubbles screams.

Bubbles: (*offstage*) No, don't . . .

The sound of a slap.

Jesus, help me.

Q: Don't any of you get it yet? That motherfucker doesn't help *anyone*. And he's not going to help you. Now open wide, motherfucker.

Bubbles cries out.

Bubbles: No, please . . .

She cries out again . . . but this time it's muffled.

Dante begins to cry.

Dante: Are we gonna die? We're gonna die, aren't we?

Tahlz: Fa'amālosi, son. Fa'amālosi.

Tahlz looks over at Si as if for the first time.

I know you.

Si: No you don't.

Tahlz: I've been trying to work it out. How I know you. You grew up round here, right?

Si: I don't know you.

Tahlz: You know Rafael, right?

Si: Rafael?

Tahlz: He's your brother, isn't he? He was in my boy's class at Tangaroa. You were a few years below, right? Simple

	Simon.
Si:	Don't call me that.

The sound of a smack.

Bubbles screams.

Q laughs.

Tahlz:	I know a lot of the kids used to call you that. But I never did. How is your brother?
Si:	He's dead.
Tahlz:	I'm sorry to hear that. He looked out for you, your brother. I remember that. He loved you. And I bet you loved him.

Si is silent.

Dante's my son. My youngest. This is his first shift here tonight. What do you think about that? I love my son, Simon. Probably like Rafael loved you. I don't want anything to happen to my son, Simon. He hasn't done anything to anyone. He's just a kid. Look at him. Simon? Please. Look at him. He's only eighteen. He's not that much younger than you? How old are you?

Si:	Twenty. When I'm twenty-one Mum said we can have a pig. Cool, eh?
Tahlz:	Will you let my son go? Please, Simon.

Silence.

You know the difference between good and bad, right, Simon? Everybody knows the difference between good and bad. Well, what I'm asking is: Will you do one good thing tonight? Please.

Bubbles screams again.

| Si: | Q won't like it. |

Tahlz:	No. He won't. But it's the right thing to do. The good thing to do. Just like when everyone was calling you Simple Simon, I knew what the right thing to do was. The good thing to do. To not call you that name. Because that name hurt. You know this is the right thing, Simon. Please, Simon. I'm begging you. Let him go. Please.

Bubbles screams again.

	Life's about choice. I truly believe that, Simon. And we are our choices. Do you understand that? The things we choose to do or not do, they define us. They make us who we are. Do you get what I'm saying?
Si:	He'll tell me off.
Tahlz:	That's okay. I'm here. I'll tell him what happened. I can just say that Dante ran outside when you weren't looking.
Si:	Yeah, but that's a lie. That's a bad thing.
Tahlz:	Sometimes—sometimes it's the right thing.
Si:	I'm getting confused.
Tahlz:	Please, Simon. Please let my son go.

Si lowers his gun.

Dante looks at Tahlz.

	Go.
Dante:	What about you?

Bubbles screams. But her scream sounds tired and worn. Final.

Tahlz:	There's no time, Dante. Don't make me say it again.
Dante:	I love you, Mum.
Tahlz:	I love you too, son.

Se vave. Before he comes back.

Dante is almost out the door when Q appears.

Q: What the fuck's going on here? Where the fuck do you think you're going?

Q grabs the gun off Si.

Si: It's her son.

Q: So?

Si: She loves her son.

Q: So what?

Si: Sorry, Q.

Q: You better toughen up, uso. You're no use to me soft. Fuck it. I'm not going out like that. This is where we're going to make our last stand. You understand that don't you, Si?

Si: What do you mean?

Q: This is it. This is the end. We're going to go out in a blaze of glory. You and me. Legendary. Give them an ending they won't forget. Be in all the papers. Be on the news. Everywhere around the world. Q and Si: Club Paradiso.

Dante joins Tahlz.

Si: I don't get it.

Q: We need to make this memorable. So what are we up to now?

Si: The cop . . . the fafa . . . the man. Three.

Q: Time for four. The lady. Or the kid. Whatever. Your turn.

Si realises Q means for him to kill Tahlz or Dante. He hesitates.

You want to know how it feels, don't you? You did before.

Silence.

You gone soft on me, Si? Can't have that, uso. Not now, uso. Now are you with me?

Si: Yes.

Q: ARE YOU WITH ME?

Si: YES.

Q produces a scary-looking knife.

Q: Then prove it.

Si looks down at the knife.

Dante: NOOOOOOOOOOO!

Tahlz: Jesus, please!

Q: I said PROVE IT.

Silence.

Si looks up at Tahlz and then at Dante.

A beat and then.

Tahlz: Run!

Tahlz and Dante bolt in opposite directions.

Q: Get the piggy wiggies. Get 'em both.

Si grabs Tahlz.

Tahlz: Dante, may God protect you.

Q: Do it! DO IT!

Dante: Please, that's my mum, please don't hurt her, please . . .

Si prepares to stab Tahlz but he can't.

Si: I can't.

Q: FUCK THAT. That is *weak*. Gimme that.

            Q grabs his knife.

Si: No, leave her, Q . . .

            *Q goes to stab Tahlz but Si steps in his path . . . and
            receives a fatal wound.*

            Si slowly falls to the ground in Q's arms.

Q: Si?

Si: Dad?

            Number four, Dad. I'm number four.

            Si dies.

            Q can't believe it.

            *For a moment he cradles Si's lifeless body in his
            arms . . . until he looks up at Tahlz.*

            He's murderous.

Q: Look at what you did.

Tahlz: You don't need to do this, Q. Please. You can choose
            not to do this. It doesn't have to end this way.

Q: Yeah, it does.

            *Tahlz begins to back away from Q as he approaches her
            with the knife.*

Tahlz: 'Our Father who Art in Heaven, hallowed be thy
            name, thy kingdom come thy will be done on earth
            as it is in heaven . . .'

Q: (*over Tahlz*) Blah blah blah. God's not going to save
            you, suga. I know that for a fact. You wanna know
            how I know that? Because, look—

            Q stabs Tahlz.

            Tahlz falls to the ground.

Dante: Noooooooooooo!

Dante flies at Q with everything he has and knocks Q off-balance.

The knife goes flying, as does the gun.

But Dante isn't nearly strong enough to overpower Q.

Q starts to strangle Dante with his bare hands . . .

. . . until Bubbles, now bloodied and bruised, staggers into the room.

She sees the knife, grabs it, comes up behind Q and stabs him.

Q is so pumped up with drugs he hardly registers the pain and backhands Bubbles.

Dante jumps on Q's back. They struggle.

Bubbles searches desperately for the gun—and finds it by Si's body. She points it at Q.

Q lets Dante go and seems resigned.

Q: Yeah. Yeah, okay. Alright. Alright.

Suddenly he lunges at Bubbles.

Bubbles shoots. And shoots. Until there are no more bullets.

Dante silently takes the gun from Bubbles.

A beat of silence.

Tahlz gasps. She's still alive.

Dante rushes to her side.

Dante: Mum? I'm here. Hold on. We're going to get help. (*to Bubbles*) Call an ambulance.

Bubbles finds her phone and dials.

I got you, Mum.

Bubbles: Hello? (*waits*) Ambulance.

Dante: I got you, Mum.

Bubbles: (*waits*) Club Paradiso. Dawson Road. Flat Bush. Yeah, that's right. Club Paradiso.

Dante: I got you.

Lights fade.

The End